GILES & SUE LIVE

THE GOOD LIFE

WITH
GILES COREN
AND
SUE PERKINS

How to go Self-sufficient in the Suburbs

BBC
BOOKS

CONTENTS

INTRODUCTION

In the past, Giles Coren and Sue Perkins have lived like Edwardians, sampled the culinary delights of historical periods from Ancient Rome to the French Revolution and eaten their way through the twenties, forties and eighties.

For *Giles and Sue Live The Good Life*, however, it was time for the many-costumed duo to come back down to earth, literally. This time they would have to sing – or at least dig – for their supper in a bid to learn some of the 1970's self-sufficiency skills and techniques, as fictionalized in the classic sitcom *The Good Life*. They wouldn't actually be living the life, but they would be discovering what it takes – all to find out whether the good life could be a reality.

Over a summer, Giles and Sue sampled the fictional lives of Tom and Barbara Good, who famously dropped out of the rat race and turned their suburban garden into a veg lovers' paradise and reared chickens, pigs and goats to provide food.

In the 35 years since the show's stars, Richard Briers and Felicity Kendal, first tugged on their wellies, the self-sufficiency movement has come full circle, with more and more disgruntled office workers packing up and moving to smallholdings to escape the pressures of city life.

In the mid seventies, when the movement first started in earnest, householders were seeking an alternative way of life for different reasons. They had lived through wartime rationing, the austerity of the 1950s and the boom years of the 1960s. After two decades of embracing new convenience and processed foods and cheaper production methods, things began to crash for UK consumers. Soaring oil prices, miners' strikes and the three-day week saw food prices rocket and inflation peaking at 25 per cent. Many began to look at alternative lifestyles and in 1973, the father of the movement, John Seymour, published *Farming for Self-Sufficiency*. Two years later, the first series of *The Good Life* coincided with the launch of *Practical Self-Sufficiency* magazine. Then, in 1976, John Seymour published his comprehensive book *The Complete Book of Self-Sufficiency*.

Subsequent decades saw the growth of supermarkets, which forced food prices down for everyday shoppers, and the movement fell out of fashion. But twenty-first century concerns over pesticides, environmental impact and genetically modified crops means that many are beginning to turn back to the grow-your-own movement, if stopping short of full self-sufficiency.

In 2009, an ICM survey of more than 1,000 people found that 26 per cent were growing their own fruit and vegetables. Three quarters of those said they were doing it to save money, although health and environmental concerns were also factors. Sales of ready-to-plant vegetables from one major DIY chain soared by 40 per cent in the same year and vegetable seed sales increased by 27 per cent.

In 1998, the first modern-day farmers' market was set up in Bath, sparking a movement towards regular markets across the country. There are now 750 farmers' markets in the UK, generating £250 million a year.

The four decades since *The Good Life* have also seen changes in methods, with pesticides and chemicals shunned by the majority of 'grow-your-own' practitioners. Livestock has changed too, with alpacas, reindeer and ostriches joining the more traditional choices of livestock. The advent of the Internet has made it far easier for potential smallholders to gather and share information, and the Web is packed with advice encouraging an earthier lifestyle.

On the flip side, the reliance on gadgets and technology in our everyday lives, plus the many compulsory bills, means that going the whole hog and supporting your family with no income has become increasingly difficult. Instead, more and more people are adopting a few of the principles of *The Good Life* while maintaining an income in order to pay bills and for essentials.

As part of the Good Life project, Giles and Sue had to grow vegetables, collect eggs from their chickens and make their own goat's cheese, bread and chutney. Speaking on the first day in the house, Giles was looking forward to putting his back into the spadework.

'I like the physical activity aspect of it,' he said. 'Getting some exercise at the same time is a real bonus. I'm really hoping that, if this stuff grows, we'll be harvesting more than we can eat so we can take it home.'

Sue had other plans for the wide variety of veg in the garden.

'I'm going to see if we can't just eat everything!' she laughed. 'Bottling and preserving sounds like just about the dullest thing you can do, but actually I am quite interested to see what we can make out of what we've got, so I'm going to be subjecting Giles to some fairly left-field recipes, mainly involving marrows. My marrow and strawberry bake is going to be something that really needs to be seen to be believed!'

For comedian and presenter Sue, the chance to eat healthily, while putting some work into the food's production was an appealing prospect after the huge meals she had to eat on the *Supersizers* series.

'What's nice about this is that we are doing it in real time rather than trying to cram a whole piece of history into a gluttonous nine days. This project started when the planting season began in March and will go through to September, when we will have harvested everything apart from our tomatoes. There's a sense of actually achieving something.'

Partner-in-grime Giles, however, was not entirely convinced he had the green fingers necessary for the job that lay ahead. 'There will be some disaster, I'm sure, because the reality is that when you grow things some stuff works and some doesn't,' he predicted. 'You can't get too excited about your broad bean salad because the broad beans might get that black disease that mine get whenever I've tried. People reading this book can flick forward to see if they have any photos of us holding large vegetables, but right now that's an advantage they have over us.'

PART ONE
GOING
SELF
SUFFICIENT

PREPARING TO LEAD THE GOOD LIFE ❀ 1

It all began when Tom Good, a loving husband and talented draughtsman, decided to opt out of the rat race. Tom's light bulb moment came on his 40th birthday, 4 April 1975, in the now-classic BBC sitcom *The Good Life*. From that day on, his loyal wife Barbara, and over 15 million viewers, joined Tom on a journey of self-sufficiency and self-discovery, under the watchful and disapproving eye of best friends and next-door neighbours Margo and Jerry Leadbetter.

Tom's first task was to convert the couple's beloved Surbiton semi and attractive lawned garden into a fully functioning, self-supporting smallholding. The garden needed to be turned into a vegetable patch and fitted out with various animal pens, and the suburban kitchen required an old cast-iron range in place of the electric oven and hob.

Thirty-five years on, another suburban semi, this time in North London, was to be turned into a Good-style homestead for two new novice 'Good Lifers' Giles Coren and Sue Perkins. The entire house needed to be restyled to reflect the interior of the Goods' cosy home, with one room doubling as the living room of Margo and Jerry.

'Normally, as a set designer, you would interpret the look yourself, but this had to be as much like the original set as possible so it's almost a replica,' says art director Carrie Southall. 'Obviously I couldn't find everything exactly the same, but I tried to find the nearest equivalent to the Goods' style.'

Although *The Good Life* is set firmly in the 1970s, the general theme of the set is not the glaring psychedelic prints and orange plastic that you might associate with the period. Tom and Barbara Good had a much more understated look, which Carrie has managed to copy to a tee.

'If you watch the show, and you see their interiors, it wasn't what you think of as being seventies,' Carrie explains. 'Their lounge was furnished with quite a few items of dark wood, the Edwardian revival furniture. They would have lived with items passed down from their families, so there were a lot of faded florals and classic wooden furniture.'

In contrast to the homely charm of the Goods' rooms, Carrie was also tasked with emulating the mock grandeur of neighbours Margo and Jerry. The lives of the Leadbetters were far more conventional for the time and Jerry's high-powered position at Tom's former company afforded them a comfortable existence. However, Margo's taste in décor was more pretentious and aspirational than her practical neighbours.

'Margo and Jerry were a little more modern, but they still didn't choose the bright orange, flowery look that you associate with the era,' Carrie points out. 'I needed to find white cherub vases and a carriage clock. Margo was going for a more pseudo-elegant look – trying to create a stately-home look in Surbiton.'

In order to emulate the couples' differing styles, Carrie trawled car boot sales, charity shops and antique shops, and sifted through Internet auction sites. Two weeks before Giles and Sue were due to embark on *The Good Life*, and armed with an impressive collection of 1970s crockery and furniture, Carrie began her transformation. Teams of builders, decorators and garden experts moved into the rented semi, and began to bring seventies Surbiton to a quiet cul-de-sac near Harrow.

The Goods' Lounge

The main reception room in Tom and Barbara's house was the lounge-diner, where the devoted couple snuggled up on the huge squashy sofa to 'watch the space where the telly used to be'. The décor was largely shabby chintz, with beige flock wallpaper and faded floral furniture, dotted with dark wood tables and white open shelving.

For Carrie, this room proved the hardest challenge.

'The set from the original programme is much bigger than the one we have and was divided by the shelves,' she said. 'It was nice to look at, but the one we have is a square box.'

Unlike the Surbiton set, the downstairs of the North London house is split into three rooms – the lounge, dining room and kitchen. The room that Giles and Sue were to use as a lounge was clad in dark wood panelling and boasted an Arts and

'The lounge was a festival of browns! We think of the seventies as this groovy decade of chic interior design and extraordinary design pieces, but actually we hadn't really evolved much from the post-war dark colours and pokey rooms. It's a bit overwhelmingly chintzy and grim rather than the shagpile carpet, Austin Powers sexfest we all wanted.'

Crafts-style tiled fireplace. The first job was to cover the wood and to paper the walls with a two-tone beige, floral damask wallpaper. The fireplace was then boxed in with fake brick stuck on to replicate the Goods' sandstone surround, a fashionable look at the time. The existing light brown carpet, by happy coincidence, was similar to the one in the original house.

In the bay window, Carrie made the dining area with a Victorian pedestal table dressed complete with the ever-present yellow tablecloth and a vase of flowers.
The sofa proved a little more difficult to track down. 'The shape of it was strange and very distinctive – the arms were flat, thin and upright with cushions on top.'

In fact, the room would be too small for the original settee so Carrie settled for a two-seater sofa and a seventies-style cabinet, stuffed with knick-knacks. And there was, of course, no eletricity-guzzling television.

Margo and Jerry's Lounge

To provide a contrast to the frugal existence of self-sufficiency, every so often Giles and Sue took on the mantle of the Leadbetters and indulged in the more frivolous world of cocktail parties and canapés. For these occasions, they moved to the second living room, a replica of Margo and Jerry's expensively furnished home.

The French doors, opening onto the garden, were the most important feature of the room as Margo was often seen on a

sun lounger sipping an aperitif, entertaining Jerry's boss on the patio or simply checking out the latest atrocity in the Good's neighbouring garden.

Carrie chose a muted, pale green flock wallpaper for the room, sourcing genuine vintage paper.

'I did look for a modern equivalent, but I couldn't find anything because the colours were too bright or there was a metallic sheen to them,' she explains. 'The seventies stuff was a bit too floral and bold so we were looking back to pre-seventies.'

The centrepiece of the room is a gold Dralon sofa, with matching recliner chair, which Carrie found on an auction site for £15. Margo-style ornaments and gold-framed pictures adorn the room and the obligatory fake wood drinks trolley, picked up at a boot sale for £5, provides a home for the cocktail shaker and whisky decanter.

'I thought Margo and Jerry's room would be much more bourgeois and aspirational, but at least they have a nice patio. I'm looking forward to lying on my Day-Glo lounger. The memorable thing about Margo and Jerry was the sheer volume of booze and cigarettes they could consume. They could turn any room brown in 20 seconds with all the filterless fags they were chuffing. Although I'm happy to try a little pea pod wine as Tom and Barbara, I'm really looking forward to Dry Vermouth by the bucketload as Margo and Jerry.'

'The two couples were polar opposites. In the 1970s, Margo and Jerry were seen as posh and sophisticated, while Tom and Barbara were mad, laugh-a-minute radicals. But now, Tom and Barbara would be viewed as much more progressive and the Margo and Jerry types would be irredeemably bourgeois.'

The Kitchen

The Goods' kitchen was the hub of the house. With the door opening directly onto their self-sufficient garden, this is where they came and went, leaving their muddy boots at the door to boil some water on the wood-burning stove for a much-needed cuppa. As well as being the place where Barbara baked, pickled and plucked, they used the kitchen to eat, plan and mull over the progress of the day.

For Giles and Sue it had to be a working kitchen, where they too would learn to bake bread, pickle eggs and make pea pod wine. The kitchen was to undergo the most radical transformation of all the rooms, mainly because of the central feature – the stove.

'The wood-burning stove has been quite a big thing, and we've had four different parties involved,' Carrie reveals. 'There's been the builders who ripped out cabinets, the guy from the stove company, the chimney man and the chimney lining people. It's been really complicated.'

Things have changed dramatically since the seventies, when Tom and Barbara bought a rusty old range and installed it themselves. Now, it has to be put on blocks, at least 40cm away from combustible material, and the pipework covered in non-combustible cladding. The sink unit, which already included the required stainless-steel sink, had to be ripped out and rebuilt because it was too close to the stove.

'In the storecupboard there were jars of lentils. Sue suggested that back then they only ate them because they were orange and they fitted in with the colour scheme.'

'The storecupboard ingredients were pretty bland and uninviting, but the idea of the stove we've rather taken to – it adds an extra element of jeopardy to the whole cooking experience.'

Elsewhere, the wall tiles were covered in the pale blue geometric wallpaper of the original series and the modern boiler was boxed in.

The plain white units in the kitchen were a good starting point for the Goods' unusual, two-tone kitchen cupboards. Carrie kept half the units and covered the doors with Fablon, a sticky-backed plastic that creates a wood effect. The other half were ripped out to make way for the huge pine dresser that Tom and Barbara had stuffed full of crockery.

'I worked out that a lot of their kitchenware was Staffordshire kiln craft and that's really hard to find,' admits Carrie. 'I managed to find four bowls on the Internet, which cost about £5, but nothing else.'

Another familiar seventies throwback dotted around the set is the brown Hornsea crockery, in the distinctive brown and orange Heirloom and Saffron patterns.

'A lot of the stuff, like the Hornsea crockery, is becoming really collectible and these were popular patterns. Loads of people had something in these designs – from the jugs and coffee cups to the storage jars with the wooden tops, which many of us still remember today. But the Goods also had the classic look, like plain white milk jugs.

'The kitchen dresser needed to be crammed full, but not just for aesthetics. It's a working kitchen, so we had to make sure there were enough bowls, plates and jugs for Giles and Sue to use.'

To save space, the large pine table around which Tom and Barbara were often seen was downsized for the new house. Completing the kitchen is an old-fashioned larder, an original feature of the house, which housed the store-cupboard essentials and a few demijohns for the homemade wine.

GETTING PRACTICAL

A Home on the Range

For Barbara and Tom Good, a wood-burning kitchen range would have meant a huge saving when it came to heating the house, producing hot water and cooking meals. In fact, in the early seventies there was a surplus of wood due to a particularly virulent strain of Dutch elm disease, which wiped out 25 million trees in the UK alone. In many areas, councils simply gave the wood away, so the range represented a way to use this free fuel to the utmost efficiency.

The stove that Giles and Sue cooked on was a 1960s 'combi', which meant it could burn coal or logs. In its full working glory, a pipe leading from the range would heat a tank of water that would store the heat until it was needed. The chamber housing the fire was well sealed and the stove would be kept burning 24 hours a day.

Today, wood-burning stoves and ranges are enjoying a revival, and many people see them as a cheaper, more efficient and aesthetically pleasing way to heat the house. However, much has changed since Tom and Barbara's day. In the seventies, the environmental movement was in its infancy and concerns over emissions and fossil fuel depletion were held by the radical few. Today, heating and cooking methods are beginning to be informed as much by the desire to save the planet as the need to reduce costs. Thanks to the Clean Air Act of 1993 (the Clean Air Act 1981 in Northern Ireland), which aims to reduce smoke emissions, Giles and Sue were actually unable to burn wood in their range as the house was situated in a Smoke Control Zone. Instead they used phurnacite coal, a smokeless fuel.

If you do not live in a Smoke Control Zone, burning wood to heat the house and for cooking is still the most environmentally-friendly option. Unlike coal or gas and electricity, which are produced in coal or nuclear power stations, wood, providing it comes from a source where trees are regularly replaced, is a renewable fuel. And the good news is that wood burned on wood-burning ranges only gives out as much carbon dioxide as it absorbed in its lifetime. Providing we continue to plant trees, this means it is carbon-neutral. And as a wood-

burning range also heats water, there is no need for a gas-guzzling boiler either.

Although the models used in the Good's house and by Giles and Sue are too old to use today, some modern solid fuel stoves are allowed to burn wood in Smoke Control Zones due to technology such as the 'clean-burn' or 'clean-heat' system. This allows them to burn an inherently smoky solid fuel without emitting smoke, making them greener still. So, when looking for a range, check to see which models are exempt from the ban and which approved fuels they can burn under the Clean Air Acts.

While wood-burning ranges are currently the greener option, coming top in surveys of energy ratings (followed by gas ovens and with electric ovens bringing up the rear), electric-oven manufacturers have also started to think green. Gas ovens fall to last place if the electricity you use to power an electric oven comes from a 'green' company or you generate your own electricity through solar panels or some other means.

New electric ovens also now come with a helpful energy-efficiency rating, so if a wood-burning range isn't for you, look for an electric oven with the top efficiency rating of A.

Energy concerns are not the only thing that has changed since the seventies, and a lot more emphasis is now put on health and safety. While Tom and Barbara merely picked up a rusty range from the scrap-metal man that someone had dumped, cleaned it up and installed it themselves, the safety regulations surrounding modern day installations are lengthy and complicated and it is strongly recommended that a registered installer is used to minimize risk of home fires. So is a wood-burning range right for you? There are some key points to consider…

The Clean Air Act 1993

Many boroughs, especially those in densely populated towns and cities, have smoke control areas. In these areas it is forbidden to burn wood or house coal, and a smokeless fuel, such as coke briquettes or fire logs, must be used. That means there's no such thing as free fuel, and the costs of running a range are now greater.

However, a number of new ranges are exempt from this ruling because they have built-in smoke reduction technology. For an up-to-date list of authorized fuels and exempted appliances for use in Smoke Control Zones, and to find out whether your home is in a Smoke Control Zone, go to the government website or contact the Department for Environment, Food and Rural Affairs, Air Quality Policy Division (see Useful Resources on page 220 for details).

Fuel sources

Where will you be buying or obtaining your fuel from? The endless supply of wood that Tom and Barbara enjoyed has now dried up and logs and other types of solid fuel can be surprisingly expensive. Factor in the transportation costs as well: you may have to travel to source your solid fuel and that could eat into the saving.

Defra (Department for Environment, Farming and Rural Affairs) guidelines state that wood products must be from renewable sources to claim low CO_2 emission values. Even if your stove is an approved or exempted model, there are strict guidelines about the type of wood that can be burnt and 'seasoned' (dried naturally for over a year), or untreated wood is recommended. Where a product runs on woodchip or wood pellets there will be manufacturer's guidelines as to the quality and type.

Fuel is also bulky and you will need a reasonably large, dry storage area not too far from the stove. If possible, keep some in the house so that you don't have to dash down to the bottom of the garden in the middle of the night for supplies.

The flue

Any solid fuel appliance requires a flue lined with a suitable material. If a chimney is already in place, it is possible to have it lined. If there is no existing chimney or flue, you will need to consider where one can be installed. Either way, the work needed may be costly. For a full list of building regulations surrounding solid fuel appliances, go to: www.planningportal.gov.uk and download Document J.

Installation

On completion of the installation, a Certificate of Compliance must be obtained. There are two ways to get one (in England and Wales):

a) Choose an installer who is registered on a government-recognized Competent Persons Scheme, such as HETAS, who can self-certify his work.

b) Have the work certified by the local authority building control department for a fee, which may be as much as £300.

The first option is strongly recommended, as a registered fitter will be aware of all the building regulations and safety requirements and will leave you with the certificate as well as forwarding a copy to HETAS, who will inform the local authority on your behalf. For registered installers see the HETAS website: www.hetas.co.uk.

If you choose to install without a registered fitter, contact your local authority before you start to make sure you can get the work certified by them and to find out how it much it will cost.

In Scotland there are different requirements and a building warrant scheme is in operation, currently administered by SBSA.

LIVING OFF THE LAND ❀ 2

When Tom decided to rip up the lawn and create a muddy paradise of personal produce, his first task was to prepare the garden. He sourced a rotary cultivator, or rotavator, and swiftly fell out with the Leadbetters when he decided to rotavate the garden at six in the morning.

The Goods had a large garden and grew a range of crops with varying effort and success. Escaping pigs destroyed their vegetables and Margo rang the death knell on their soft fruit crop when she insisted on putting up a windbreak that cut out all their sun. Planting seed potatoes was a particularly arduous task and to avoid the traditional, back-breaking method, Tom invented the 'Non-Stoop Good-O-Scope'. While it dropped the potatoes into the hole without him having to bend, it dropped them upside down. By the time they had finished re-planting the potatoes, Tom didn't even have the energy to take off his wellies.

Preparing and Planting

In terms of the basic advice for growing fruit and vegetables, little has changed in the last 40 years. The preparation remains the same, as does the rotation of the crops. In his 1977 book, *How to Grow Vegetables and Fruit,* legendary gardener Percy Thrower wrote that soil preparation was 'the biggest single factor in a successful vegetable production'. Chatting to Giles and Sue, *Gardeners' World* presenter Joe Swift echoed his sentiment: 'Prepare the area properly before planting. Dig quite deep, turn the soil over, get all the roots out to stop weeds taking over the plot.'

In keeping with *The Good Life* spirit, Giles had a go at rotavating the garden (although he waited until midday to start up the noisy contraption). He soon turned the front lawn into a large planting bed, with three more beds in the back garden. The impressive machine tore up the grass and loosened soil, which would have taken an age to dig.

In the Goods' day, before fears over foot and mouth and other diseases, a cheaper and more eco-friendly alternative was to borrow a pig or two. They would not only churn up the garden, but would also eat every root in sight. For modern-day conversions, a rotavator presents a far more viable option.

Once the garden was rotavated, the roots taken out and the soil brought up to standard, it was time to get planting. The next step was to choose the fruit and veg that the two presenters would be living on. The 1975 seed catalogue they pored over was actually remarkably similar to the 2010 version, especially in terms of favourite varieties. Eight out of 20 of the top-selling seeds haven't changed, with the same type of peas, radishes and carrot still the top choice of many UK gardeners. The 2010 best seller – beetroot 'Boltardy' – was in second place in 1975, although the former number one – runner bean 'Scarlet Emperor' – has now slipped out of the top 20. The area that has altered most is the salad leaves, with the classic British favourite 'Webbs Wonderful' giving way to more exotic salads, such as rocket, as well as mixed lettuce leaves and basil.

'One of the problems with this gardening lark is that I have a reputation as a peachy-skinned urban sophisticate to protect. If I end up all wind-chapped and horny-handed with muddy fingernails, I simply won't be able to show my face in the elegant salons of Mayfair.'

Giles planted courgettes and pumpkins for the front garden along with 15 strawberry plants and some broad beans. For the back garden, 'Webbs Wonderful', along with a wide variety of veg including potatoes, beans, peas, carrots, onions, garlic and lettuce were planted. Planting enough in the garden for everyday needs would mean fewer trips to the allotment, where larger quantities of similar crops were planted.

A long winter meant everything was planted a few weeks later than the desired date, and even then a few beans were lost to a late frost. To stagger the harvest, they chose three types of potatoes, all classic seventies varieties – first earlies ('Duke of York'), late earlies ('Lady Christl') and lates ('Jersey Royal').

First earlies are new potatoes that are planted at Easter. Traditionally, you are supposed to prepare the ground on Easter Friday, plant them on Easter Sunday and in 8–12 weeks you will have your first crop. Late earlies are planted at the same time as earlies, but take 2–3 weeks longer to mature. Lates are planted towards the end of April, weather permitting, and take about 20 weeks to grow.

'When I lived in Cornwall, I grew quite a few veg, but I made a lot of mistakes. You've got to love the seed. I don't mean sing songs to them and talk to them in a Prince Charles kind of way – who's got time for that, other than a member of the royal family? But you do have to make sure they're all right.'

Although they were not producing as much food as the Goods, Sue acknowledged that growing your own is hard work indeed: 'I grow quite a lot, but what this experiment shows is that you need quite a bit of free time. You can't be a veg dilettante – you can't just bung them in the ground and expect nature to do her magic. You do have to check the soil is the right pH, you have to fertilize the plant and water it, and you have to make sure that no predators get to it.

'It's quite hardcore, but what I hope we show is that it is worth it, that the end result is better than what you would get at a supermarket. You feel good about yourself and it is a great hobby.'

By the first week of June, two months after planting out the veg in the garden, Giles and Sue were already reaping the rewards with the first crop of radishes. They also had a visit from real Good Lifers Dennis and Patricia Cleveland-Peck, who gave them some useful pointers on their potato patch.

'Our visitant Good Lifers pointed out that our potatoes were showing too much leaf, so we had to put more compost over them. The potatoes were planted in little furrows, and I'd always wondered why, so we knocked the tops off the furrows to cover them.

When we've finished, I imagine the amount of potatoes we'll have will make a small bowl of potato salad. If it came to some sort of global thermonuclear Armageddon and Sue and I had to go into hiding underneath the pig shelter, we would be able to survive, possibly, for an afternoon. After that, we would have to go shopping.'

Preparing the Soil

Before you begin to plant, find out what you're dealing with so you can make the most of the soil you have and add the correct nutrients. These days, a soil-testing kit is available for a few pounds from garden centres and DIY stores. Otherwise, the old-fashioned method still stands. Grab a handful of soil, sift it through your fingers and try to make it into a ball. It should fit into one of the following categories:

Clay: This is the type of soil in Giles and Sue's garden. Sticky and heavy, it can easily be formed into a ball shape. Although packed with nutrients, it bakes hard in the summer and tends to get waterlogged in the winter, so it's difficult to dig. Use plenty of organic matter and keep it well dug.

Chalky: Particularly common in the south-east of England, this soil type contains lumps of chalk and flint, which makes digging down difficult. It is also alkaline and needs to be constantly watered.

Sandy: A rough, gritty, sandy brown colour soil that won't be moulded into shapes. It has good drainage and is quick to warm up, so spring planting can be a little earlier. Needs lots of water in hot weather.

Silty: Often found near rivers, the tiny particles mean it is silky to the touch. Plenty of nutrients and good drainage.

Peaty: Dark, spongy soil, often with a high acid content, which some crops will react against. Stays wet in winter, but can dry out too much in the summer.

Loamy: The jackpot for vegetable growers! This fertile, brown, crumbly earth is high in nutrients and drains perfectly, rarely becoming waterlogged. Almost anything can grow in it and it's easy to dig. Avid gardeners can achieve something similar with regular digging and a whole heap of manure and compost.

pH Levels

A soil-testing kit will also test the pH level of your soil. Seven is neutral and fantastic for most vegetables. Below seven is acidic and best for root veg such as swede and radishes, as well as potatoes. Above seven is alkaline, favoured by brassicas such as cabbage and cauliflower. If the soil is too acidic, the veg may suffer so you might want to add garden lime to bring up the pH. If you want to bring the alkaline level down, add

'Soil pH? Who in the world can be bothered with that? I would literally buy some tomato plants, dig a hole, whack them in, water them once then go off on holiday and come back saying, "Where's the salad?"'

manure or sulphur. Ideally, when using manure, it should be dug in during the autumn, ready for spring planting.

Crop Rotation

To get the maximum benefit out of small vegetable plots, a four-year rotation is recommended. This ensures that the crops don't take the same nutrients from the soil year after year, and you avoid a build-up of plant-specific pests. Some plants also put nutrients back into the soil, ready for those that need more than their fair share.

Ideally, split the crops into four categories: roots, brassicas, legumes and others. Then rotate the crops in the following pattern:

	Year 1	Year 2	Year 3	Year 4
Plot 1	Legumes	Others	Brassicas	Roots
Plot 2	Brassicas	Legumes	Roots	Others
Plot 3	Roots	Brassicas	Others	Legumes
Plot 4	Others	Roots	Legumes	Brassicas

Note: Sweetcorn, chicory, courgette, lettuce, peppers, pumpkins, asparagus and rhubarb can be planted in any of the beds.

'I love the idea of growing my own produce, but in reality I wouldn't want to drive somewhere to do the gardening. If it's out the back of the house, marvellous. But once you're getting in the car you might as well go to the greengrocer's.

The Allotment

With Giles and Sue working on a garden plot barely half the size of the original Surbiton utopia, they maximized their crop by taking on an allotment as well. They were able to secure a full plot for the duration of the programme, in a miraculously short time and just a short drive away from the north London semi. Most potential allotmenteers are not so lucky – a recent survey found that 94,124 people are on waiting lists in England alone.

Joe Swift, who chronicled his own progress on an allotment for a year, explains: 'Most areas have huge waiting lists; in some areas it's 10–15 years. They vary wildly in rent. Up north I found someone who is paying something like £7 a year, but most are about £30–£40. In London they are a bit more expensive – mine was about £65.'

While Giles and Sue doubled their growing space, it also meant a doubled workload, with more digging, weeding and planting to be done. Giles managed to get out to the plot in April to work on the beds and plant the broad beans and potatoes. He then made the great mistake of leaving the plot until early June.

Allotment ace Joe was horrified with the weeds and told Giles and Sue that a visit once every couple of months is far from acceptable. And he warned that busy lives and allotments are no perfect pairings.

'The allotment is proof positive that you actually have to do a little bit of weeding occasionally. We arrived and it was basically a thicket with a few potatoes in the middle. We had two options – clear away the weeds or set fire to the whole lot and hope we got a few chips. We decided to opt for the former and it's looking a little bit better now, but it is a lesson for anyone with an allotment. You can't just take it lightly.'

'Time is something you do need a lot of, which is why it suits retired people so well,' he advised. 'People who haven't got a job to worry about always make the best allotmenteers. For a full plot you need at least a day a week. But for starters, it's better to take a quarter or, at maximum, a half. It's less daunting.'

And he had more sound advice for the beginner. 'To start, get an area of it sorted, get it planted up so it only needs weeding and watering, then move on to the next area. Don't try and do the whole thing at once, especially if you are new to gardening, because it is hard work and a lot of people put their back out within ten minutes. Once you get into shape it's wonderful, but nobody should be under the illusion that it's easy or that you can get away with planting it up in spring and going back months later for the crop.'

As well as the potatoes and broad beans, sweetcorn, courgettes, shallots, Swiss chard, carrots, beetroot and kohlrabi were planted at the allotment. For a new plot, particularly one that has not been dug for a while, Joe suggests potatoes as a great starter crop to try.

'If the soil hasn't been dug for a while, you have to dig the soil three times to harvest the potatoes – once for putting in, once for "earthing up", [when you build mounds of earth around the growing plants] and once for harvesting. So you've broken up the soil three times. Then try some easy things to grow, like courgettes; you plant one or two courgette plants and they will produce courgettes all summer long.

'Carrots and onions are great, but you have to give a certain amount of your plot over to them and you don't really see any rewards for the next six months. So it's about trying to get a good balance.

'Fruit bushes are very easy – you can plant raspberry bushes, try some apple trees, and strawberries are quite easy. Like many things, you get out of it what you put into it. It's as simple as that.'

Having been ticked off about their neglect of the plot, Giles and Sue got down to the serious business of weeding. And they had none of the weed-busting chemical sprays that the Goods may well have used in the seventies. In today's organic idyll, Joe strongly believes there's no substitute for good old-fashioned hard work.

'I would recommend hand-weeding, every time,' he says. 'The most effective way of doing it is to get in there and pull them out. Prepare the area properly before planting, dig quite deep, turn the soil over, get all the roots out. Then every time you see a weed, pull it out. You have to keep on top of it. It's about being regular and getting up to your plot as often as possible to keep on top of it. If you let it go for two or three weeks, it gets a bit out of control.'

For one area, which had overgrown entirely, Giles was keen to try another organic, if not entirely green, option – the flame thrower. 'Some gardeners will use fire to get rid of a large patch of weeds,' explains Joe. 'But I still prefer to dig them up.'

Giles, however, was soon singeing the hell out of the thistles and tall grass in the corner of the allotment.

What was Planted and Where

The majority of the plants grown in Giles and Sue's garden and allotment were also available in 1975, apart from kohlrabi 'Lanro' and courgette 'Atena', which are modern varieties, but look the same as the 1975 ones. Overleaf is a table of all the crops planted in the front and back gardens of the house and the allotment. They can all still be bought today from good garden centres.

	Plant variety	Description	When to harvest
Front garden	Broad beans: 'Suttons'	1975 dwarf variety, prolific	Early June for small beans or late June at 13cm
	Courgette: 'Atena'	Reliable, modern variety that looks like 1975 'Mont d'Or'	July/August
	Strawberries: 'Elsanta'	A popular variety for its yield and taste.	Mid July/August
Back garden bed 1	Potatoes: 'Red Duke of York'	A reliable early	Late June
	'Lady Christl'	A 1996 variety but disease-resistant late early	Early July
	'Jersey Royal'	A classic late	Mid July
Back garden bed 2	Beetroot: 'Boltardy'	Slow to start. A new variety in the 1970s	July (or earlier for baby beetroot)
	Carrots: 'Amsterdam'	High quality with deep orange crop	Both ready in July (or earlier for baby carrots)
	'Early Nantes'	A fast-maturing classic	
	French beans, climbing	Standard variety also used in 1975	Late June/early July
	Onions: 'Rijnsburger'	A good all-rounder	From August onwards
	Peas: 'Feltham First'	Very old variety, early crop	Mid June
	'Early Onward'	Heirloom variety, prolific	Mid June, sometimes earlier
	Runner beans: 'Painted Lady'	1855 variety with pretty red and white flowers	Late June/July
	Shallots: 'Drittler White Nest'	An old variety with tasty bulbs	From July
	Spring onion: 'White Lisbon'	A standard, reliable onion	Late May/early June

	Plant variety	Description	When to harvest
Back garden bed 3	Cabbage: 'Greyhound'	Pointed summer cabbage, fast grower	Mid/late July
	Chard: 'Fordhook Giant'	Grows up to 60cm tall. 1934 USA variety, seen in UK from 1975	May
	Garlic: 'Solent Wight'	Ideal for a British climate	Harvest from July
	Lettuce: 'Webbs Wonderful'	Classic iceberg lettuce	Mid June
	Radish: 'French Breakfast'	A classic radish	Late June
	Chard: 'Swiss'	Deep green leaves	Nine weeks after planting
Allotment	Broad beans: 'Bunyards Exhibition' 'Kelvedon Wonder'	Very old, tall plant with a long pod Dwarf, high yield	Mid June for both varieties
	French beans: 'Valdor'	Modern, reliable dwarf variety	July
	Lettuce: 'All Year Round' 'Lobjoits'	Classic, reliable butterhead lettuce A golden oldie with dark green heart	Mid June for both varieties
	Peas: 'Kelvedon Wonder'	Dwarf, high yield	July
	Potato: 'Jersey Royal'	A classic late	Mid July
	Runner beans: 'Enorma' 'Streamline'	20 inch long pods, large plant, high yield Reliable old variety, high yield	July for both varieties
	Tomatoes: 'Moneymaker' 'Gardeners' Delight' 'Red Alert' 'Marmande'	Smooth, medium-sized fruit. Tangy bite-sized fruit Heavy-yielding outdoor tomato Cushion shaped, large fruit	Harvest all varieties in July

The Organic Movement

Although Barbara and Tom's chosen path was more about a lifestyle change than the seemingly more modern motivations of saving the planet or having a healthier diet, there was an interest in living organically well before the Goods opted out of the rat race.

The organic movement started in the 1940s, when a few forward-thinking farmers founded the Soil Association. They had been inspired by Lady Eve Balfour, a pioneering English farmer and the first woman to study agriculture at university, who in 1939 published the results of a scientific comparison of organic and chemical farming called the 'Haughley Experiment'. She then embarked on a series of lectures and talks around farmers' markets, advocating the benefits of organic farming. She was often accompanied by Dinah Williams, who founded the UK's first organic dairy farm in Wales, now the source of Rachel's Organic dairy range.

By the 1970s the organic movement was gaining strength and had a firm supporter in the father of self-sufficiency, John Seymour, who claimed 'any fool can keep disease at bay simply by dousing his crop in chemicals'.

But this was the era of DDT (dichlorodiphenyltrichloroethane) and even mainstream garden experts like Percy Thrower advocated chemical use. In his book, *How to Grow Vegetables and Fruit*, he gave a long list of the best pesticides to use including Derris, DDT, naphthalene and gamma-HCH. The synthetic pesticide DDT was by far the most popular, and the most controversial, of the chemicals used in the 1970s. Used to control malaria and typhus in the Second World War, it began to be used as an agricultural pesticide in the late forties, as well as by gardeners, and its production soared. From 1950 to 1980, more than 40,000 tonnes were used each year worldwide and it has been estimated that a total of 1.8 million tonnes of DDT have been produced globally since the 1940s.

In 1962, biologist Rachel Carson published *Silent Spring*, challenging the use of DDT and questioning its effects on the ecosystem and on human health. She believed chemical

pesticides were a threat to wildlife, particularly birds, and could cause cancer. She was attacked by chemical companies and the US government, but she stood her ground, testifying in Congress in 1963. Her book caused a public outcry, which resulted in the banning of DDT in the US in 1972. It wasn't banned in the UK until 1984.

Pests and Diseases

Unlike Barbara and Tom, 21st-century Good Lifers Sue and Giles went for a more modern approach to gardening, under Joe Swift's guidance.

Mother Nature has her own way of controlling pests and providing you put the right plants together and follow a few handy tips, you can keep your crops organic and safe from blight. A common mistake is sticking to vegetables. Flowers are great at encouraging insects, which will eat your aphids, so don't be afraid to add some colour to your allotment.

'Plant marigolds, calendula, perennial wallflower or any plants with a nice open flower so that insects can easily access

pollen,' advises Joe Swift. 'If you grow flowers alongside your crops, rather than getting too mono-cultural, it encourages bees, which are very important, and also things like ladybirds, hover flies and lacewings that feed off aphids. It's all about increasing the levels of biodiversity and getting things to eat each other, rather than having to spray them.'

When it comes to birds, a scarecrow is one organic solution. In *The Good Life* Barbara upset Margo by using her hand-me-down clothes to keep the feathered fiends at bay. Giles and Sue paid tribute to the formidable Mrs Leadbetter with their own allotment scarecrow.

Common Pests and Green Solutions

Aphids: An infestation of black fly or other aphid can be cleared with ordinary washing-up liquid. Spray soapy water onto the leaves or put some on your hands and wipe the aphids off. Aphids breathe through the skin, so the soapy water asphyxiates them and won't harm precious ladybirds.

Carrot root fly: This common nemesis of the carrot grower lays its eggs at the base of carrot leaves and its grubs burrow down to eat the root. Luckily the fly is easily stopped in its tracks, due to a design fault on its part – it can't fly more than about 5cm off the ground. Joe explained that experienced growers plant their carrots just off the ground, either in pots or raised beds, or they erect a barrier. Any physical barrier – fleece, cardboard or polythene about 45cm high – around the crop will stop the flies. As they are attracted by smell, especially when carrots are being thinned out, planting onions between them can mask the carrot scent and will also deter onion fly in the same way.

A greenfly infestation – you can get rid of them easily.

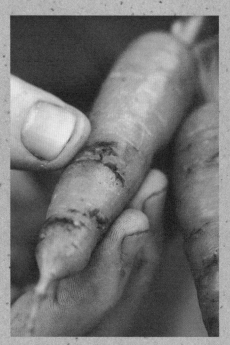

Damage caused by carrot root fly.

Slugs and snails: Slugs and snails are the vegetable grower's number one problem. Again, the natural methods are the best way of controlling them. Joe suggests organisms called nematodes that you can buy, mix with water and water in, which will eat the slugs and snails. Or you can use organic methods like beer traps, which are little pots of beer sunk into the ground. They go for the beer, fall in it and die drunk and happy! Comfrey (see page 56) mulched around your plants will stop them, as will gravel. A copper band around pots or beds will also keep them out.

Birds: Birds, especially pigeons, tend to go for your brassicas and they know precisely when things like sweetcorn are ripe. The solution is to build fruit cages, which surround the crops with netting, or to put up bird scarers, a huge range of which you can buy at garden centres.

Cover crops with netting to deter birds.

Slug damage.

Cats: Back in the Good Life garden Sue's lettuces were suffering because the local cats were using the bed as a toilet. Her solution was to knit a 'cat's cradle' of twine over the area and to erect 'a picture of one majorly ugly Schnauzer!'

'I was planting lettuces and kneeling in all this cat effluence,' said the disgusted presenter. 'It's the most toxic substance on the planet. I just reek of it!'

Sue's attempt to keep cats off her lettuces.

Take Comfort in Comfrey

Comfrey may be regarded as a weed to many, but to the knowledgeable allotment owner this versatile plant is a godsend. It is packed with nutrients and speeds up the rotting process, so it does wonders for your compost heap. Its rough foliage puts slugs and snails off so it's a perfect leaf to mulch around your plants. The leaves feed potato plants and it makes the most incredible liquid fertilizer.

'Every organic garden or allotment should have a comfrey plant next to the compost heap, or somewhere you can't see it too well,' explains Joe Swift. 'It grows in large clumps. It is amazing stuff. However, the self-seeding variety can spread like wildfire, so the best one to get is Bocking 14, which doesn't seed. If you want another plant, cut a little bit of root off and plant it in a pot.'

The large comfrey leaves make a perfect lining for potato trenches, rotting down to provide extra nourishment. You can even feed the foliage to chickens. To make comfrey fertilizer all you need is a bucket or dustbin, some leaves and some water. But Joe has a couple of words of warning.

'The liquid feed is brilliant but never put it straight onto a plant you are planning to eat. I put it all over my broccoli once and it didn't taste too good. Water around the base of the plant, and make sure you cover the container you make the mix in. After a couple of weeks it stinks like hell!'

JOE'S COMFREY FERTILIZER RECIPE

1. Chop or tear enough comfrey leaves to fill a plastic dustbin or bucket one-quarter full.

2. Top up with water and cover.

3. Leave for four weeks then dip your watering can into the liquid magic and give your soil a treat.

SOPHIE GRIGSON'S COURGETTE AND HERB RISOTTO

900ml–1.2litres (1½ –2 pints chicken or vegetable stock
60g (2oz) butter
1 onion, chopped
600g (1lb 5oz) courgettes
1 tablespoon extra virgin olive oil
225g (8oz) risotto rice (such as Arborio, Carnaroli or Vialone Nano)
150ml (5fl oz) white wine
2 tablespoon each chopped fresh parsley, basil, chives and mint
½ tablespoon chopped fresh tarragon
Salt and freshly ground black pepper
30g (1oz) Parmesan, freshly grated

1. Place the stock into a large pan over a medium heat and bring to the boil, then turn the heat down as low as it will go, to keep the stock hot, but without letting it reduce too much.

2. Heat 30g (1oz) of the butter in a wide pan over a low to moderate heat. When the butter is foaming, add the onion.

3. Using a grater, coarsely grate one-third of the courgettes. Add the grated courgettes to the pan with the onion and fry gently, without browning, until both are tender. (Sophie used new potatoes on the programme as well as courgettes because Giles and Sue didn't have quite enough courgettes and it worked just as well for this recipe.)

4. Melt 15g (½oz) of the butter with the olive oil in a frying pan over a high heat. Chop the remaining courgettes into 1cm (¼in) cubes. Add the chopped courgettes to the pan with the butter and olive oil and sauté over a medium to high heat, until they're tender and beginning to turn brown. Remove from the pan and keep warm.

5. Add the rice to the pan with the onion and grated courgettes and stir for 30–60 seconds to mix the ingredients together well. The rice should become translucent.

6. Pour in the white wine and simmer until the wine is absorbed.

7. Season the risotto with salt and pepper. When the wine is absorbed, add a ladleful of the hot stock and keep stirring, until it has been absorbed. Keep adding the stock in the same way, stirring continuously, for 20 minutes or until the rice is cooked *al dente* (tender, but still with a slight resistance to the bite). If you run out of stock before the rice is cooked, add extra boiled water. At this point, the risotto should still be fairly wet, and moist, but not swimming about in a lake of liquid.

8. When the rice is cooked, stir in the sautéed courgettes (and new potatoes if you are using them) and most of the chopped herbs (keeping aside a little for sprinkling over the final dish) into the risotto and cook for a further 1–2 minutes to heat through.

9. Finally, stir in the last of the butter and the Parmesan. Season to taste with salt and freshly ground black pepper and serve, sprinkled with the reserved chopped herbs.

SOPHIE GRIGSON'S
PEA AND MINT SOUP

....

½ onion, chopped
A little butter or oil
250g (9oz) shelled fresh peas
A small handful mint leaves
A handful or radishes
500ml (¾ pint) vegetable stock
Salt and freshly ground black
   pepper

To serve
Soft, fresh goat's cheese

1. Fry the onion gently in the butter or oil until tender. Add the peas, and radishes, cover the pan and cook over a low heat for 5 minutes.

2. Now add the stock, salt and pepper and about ⅓ of the mint leaves. Bring up to the boil, then reduce heat and simmer for 2 minutes.

3. Draw off the heat, stir in half the remaining mint leaves and then liquidize or rub through a sieve. Taste and adjust the seasoning, then serve the soup sprinkled with the remaining mint leaves and topped with a teaspoon or two of soft, fresh goat's cheese.

ANIMAL HUSBANDRY ❀ 3

Unless you're a vegan, there's more to self-sufficiency than growing veg in the garden, as Tom and Barbara knew only too well. The need for eggs, dairy products and meat meant that a large part of the garden had to be given over to animals – much to Margo's oft-voiced disgust.

But Geraldine the goat, Pinky and Perky the pigs and 12 broody hens were essential additions to the Goods' social experiment and despite the dramas, the great escapes and the worry, they were cheap to feed and gave back a great deal more than they cost.

Just like the Goods, Giles and Sue were joined at their little homestead by pigs, goats and hens. But with changing laws and stricter regulations on keeping farm animals, they soon found that animal husbandry is a lot more difficult and expensive than it was in the seventies…

Say Little Hen

Before receiving any guests of the feathered or furred variety, the suburban garden had to be converted into a haven for farm animals. The first step was to assemble the chicken coop. When it was securely fixed together, it was time for a drastic overhaul by Sue. With some bright pink paint and the addition of a pin-up of a dreamy rooster, the poultry palace was ready and Sue excitedly awaited the arrival of her new feathered friends. Meat-lover Giles, meanwhile, was left to consider the thorny issue of whether they would become Sunday lunch at any point during the show, while Sue was adamant that these birds would not see the inside of an oven.

'There'll be no animal slaughter on my watch, that's for sure. The animals are going to be treated well and kindly. It will show that they have real benefit for us psychologically and for the garden generally.'

The coop, which was placed at the end of the garden, was really only used at night and for laying. During the day, a ramp allowed them access to the living quarters where they could use one of the three nesting boxes should they want to lay an egg. The rest of the time the hens would be scratching about on the

'Fresh eggs in the morning were the gastronomic highlight of the whole thing, but I was glad I had Sue there to farm the chickens for me. I simply wasn't up to the job. Terrifying little blighters they are. *Jurassic Park* showed how birds are related to dinosaurs – and these savage beasts are first cousins of Tyrannosaurus Rex.

A VERY BRITISH COOP....

DANGER
Chickens
at work

A VERY BRITISH COOP....

lawn, a large area of which was fenced off, taking care to leave the nesting boxes outside the perimeter so that the eggs could be collected easily.

The four Light Sussex hens, delivered by expert breeder Fred Hams, are good layers, with each one expected to lay up to 260 eggs a year. The breed is renowned for being an excellent dual-purpose hen, meaning it provides a large amount of eggs as well as being a good 'table' chicken. Fred has kept chickens for 70 years and is a leading authority on the Light Sussex. His breed are the oldest line in Britain and were a popular choice in the seventies.

'Chickens are worth much more in the garden alive than dead. You get eggs from them every day, great manure from their poo (that will make your veg grow) and they are stress-bustingly, brilliant, sweet little things that chirrup around and make you happy.'

'The Light Sussex evolved between 1850 and 1900 to provide London with meat, which was very expensive. By the 1930s meat was getting cheaper and hens were expected to each lay 200 eggs a year. The pure breed is quite rare now because most breeders breed hybrids. A hybrid is massively efficient and can lay over 300 eggs a year, but it converts its food so well into eggs that it has no body weight.'

On arrival, one escapee enjoyed a quick run around the garden with Sue in hot pursuit, but, with a little help from Fred, she finally got to grips with the birds, albeit tentatively.

'I'm still getting over the whole picking them up thing, which is quite difficult,' she admitted. 'They are a combination of strong and delicate, so if you don't handle them correctly they start to squawk a bit. I don't like getting them stressed because you can feel their heart pounding underneath a terribly thin ribcage.'

But Fred was on hand to show her how to tip the hen gently on one side in your hands to calm her down. 'Once you turn them onto their side you can feel them settling down, you can feel their heartbeat slowing, just underneath your fingers,' said Sue. 'But actually I do wish I was better at catching them because I know we're stressing them out.'

Despite their initial bids for freedom, the hens happily settled into their new home. Within a few hours the first egg had appeared and Sue had given them all names. 'I called them Kerry, Susan, Germaine and Theresa – after Kerry Katona, Susan Sontag, Germaine Greer and Theresa May.

GETTING PRACTICAL

Choosing Your Chicken

During the war and throughout the 1950s, when eggs and meat were rationed, it became commonplace for Londoners to keep chickens. Chickens were cheap to feed, existing mainly on grass and kitchen scraps, and any extra eggs could be swapped for other food.

'London exported something called Tottenham Pudding to farmers to feed their chickens on during rationing. This was mostly kitchen scrapings, along with bomb-damaged goods, camp waste and restaurant waste,' explains Fred. 'Everyone had so little food to spare that every scrap was precious.'

Tom and Barbara reared their own little brood on leftovers and even scrounged Margo's shepherd's pie, or 'rustic pot roast', as she preferred to call it, leaving her enraged when she discovered it had gone to the hens rather than her needy neighbours. But much has changed since then and recent Defra guidelines state that plate scrapings should no longer be fed to animals, which makes feeding a lot more expensive.

Even so, keeping hens is a great first step towards self-sufficiency. What could be

**LEFT TO RIGHT:
Light Sussex,
Rhode Island Red
and Dorking
chicken breeds.**

better than fresh eggs every morning? There are fewer regulations than with larger animals and hens do not need to be registered, unless you have more than 50.

Here is a quick guide to the things that need to be taken into consideration when starting out:

Know your breed

Even back in the seventies, hybrids were becoming more common than the pure-bred 'dual-purpose' hens. Self-sufficiency guru John Seymour wrote: 'As a self-supporter you will want old-fashioned broody hens… You will have to search for those marvellous breeds, which can live outdoors, lay plenty of eggs, go broody and hatch their eggs, rear their chicks and make good table birds.'

Light Sussex, Rhode Island Reds and Dorking are among the best dual-purpose hens. And of course if you want to breed from them, you'll need a cockerel.

Choose your hen house carefully

There are many ready-made hen houses on the market, but although they are legal, Fred doesn't think they are all suitable. 'An ever-increasing number of households are now keeping chickens. Unfortunately, some of them are being kept in houses that allow them less room than the enhanced battery cage.

'As long as the run they have during the daylight hours is big enough, the hen house needn't be huge, but the perches must be the right distance apart. Light Sussex need a foot [30cm] of space between them, taking into account how much they hang over the perch when they're on them.'

'If you have space, the best place is a walk-in shed, with plenty of room. I like the idea of a step up and down for them. Some places do a house where the chickens live upstairs and you can move the whole house onto a fresh piece of grass.'

To comply with Defra guidelines, the horizontal distance between perches must be at least 30cm and the horizontal distance between the perch and the wall must be at least 20cm. If you are using different levels, there should be no more than four and the headroom between the levels must be at least 45cm.

For housed chickens, the stocking density must not exceed nine laying hens per square metre of usable area.

Nesting boxes are essential for laying. There should be a minimum of one box per seven birds, but more are preferable. If your hen house is a small one, make sure the boxes are easy accessible for egg collection.

eating and scratching around in the grass. Space to run in the sunlight keeps them fit, healthy and less prone to diseases. Ideally, you should be able to move the run around the garden occasionally to give them access to fresh grass. They also need an area where they can create a dust bath, as this keeps them free of fleas.

For maximum sunlight and movement, make the walls of the run as high as you can and give them a bird table or a step to jump on to. Sue and Giles also hung a cabbage at chicken head height in the run to give the birds an extra object to peck at. This helps prevent boredom, which can lead to the ladies turning on each other and literally being hen-pecked.

Give them plenty of ventilation and room to get dry

Sue's prettying up of the basic hen house worked a treat for the garden, but it had one flaw – the net curtain, which was removed on Fred's advice.

'The two things that chickens hate the most is wet and lack of ventilation,' Fred told her. 'The more ventilation they have the better.'

Sue was philosophical about the change. 'Sometimes design has to take second place to decent ventilation and animal welfare,' she reasoned.

Allowing them space to run and room to dry should they get wet is vital to their health. 'If the perches are too close together they can't get dry,' explained Fred. 'They come from an arid part of the world so they don't like to be wet. They are terribly prone to respiratory problems, but otherwise they're pretty tough.'

Allow plenty of outside space

When it comes to the area available to hens during the daylight hours, the bigger the better. A chicken gets a quarter of its food and a large proportion of its protein from

Feeding

The next-door neighbours' table scraps are now off the menu for chickens, but vegetables can still be boiled up to feed poultry, providing they don't come into contact with any animal protein. As hens are naturally omnivorous, Fred feels that this can create problems in itself, unless they have plenty of grass to peck at.

'Chickens evolved from jungle fowl that got their essential 18 per cent protein from seeds and insects, and even the smallest of mice, although it mostly came from invertebrates,' he explains. 'We used to feed 5–10 per cent fishmeal, but that is now massively expensive and has to be kept separate from other animal feed. Chickens can suffer from animal protein deprivation, so the two things that enhance their wellbeing, apart from exercise and daylight, are the capacity to find insects and quality grass to eat.'

In Barbara and Tom's day, fish was plentiful and cheap, so fishmeal was a viable feeding option. For the programme, Sue had a go at making fishmeal under Fred's instruction. What she made, however,

For entertainment, Giles and Sue hung a cabbage in the chicken pen and gave them corn on the cob to peck at.

would actually be illegal in an ordinary kitchen, but not a TV studio, as anything that is cooked in a kitchen cannot be fed to livestock. Any feed for livestock must be cooked in a separate, Defra approved area.

Another point to consider, is that between the early seventies and the turn of the century the number of adult fish living on the bed of the North Sea dropped by 90 per cent. As a result, a debate is currently raging about the environmental impact of feeding fishmeal to chickens, with many groups claiming it should be banned to help stop further depletion of fish stocks. To maintain organic status, EU regulations state that poultry should only be fed fish from sustainable sources. Some societies, such as the Soil Association, recommend that only meal made from 'offcuts' or natural by-products of the fishing industry should be used.

But don't worry, there are other ways to give your chickens the protein they need. If you don't fancy fishmeal or cannot get hold of it from a reputable source, then buy hen pellets and opt for an organic range to avoid any hidden extras.

Lettuce, cabbage leaves, corn on the cob, grain and vegetable peelings are good food for the chickens. They will also need plenty of fresh water every day.

Beware of the fox

In the forties, as suburban gardens with low fences grew in popularity, the fox population quadrupled. Since then, numbers have continued to rise and urban foxes have become increasingly bold, presenting a huge threat to chickens.

Locking your hens in a secure house at night will go some way to protecting them, but it is a myth that foxes only hunt at night so you need to protect them during daylight hours as well. Electric fences are common on more large-scale poultry farms, but if that seems too extreme then a high fence with a roof may be the answer.

'In an ideal world the chicken would have a run of the whole garden,' says Fred. 'But keeping the chicken at home and the fox out is the hardest part so a run with a roof on it is useful.'

Getting the Goat

Goats have always been a favourite animal of self-sufficient households, as they are traditionally cheap to feed and yield plenty of returns for their upkeep. With an average British Alpine milker producing 5.7 litres (12 pints) of milk a day, one goat can provide enough milk, cheese, butter and yoghurt for a family, with plenty left over to sell or barter.

British sitcom's most famous goat, Geraldine, was treated like a member of the family by the Goods, despite Tom being the butt of the joke, literally, on many occasions. In the absence of a dog, Barbara took her for walks and once set her on a leek thief with the command to 'Kill!'

In reality, the Goods made a fundamental error with Geraldine in not giving her a companion. Goats are often thought of as solitary creatures, but in fact they are herd animals and, if left alone, can begin to misbehave. Had Geraldine had a pal, Tom's buttocks may have escaped many a battering!

To help her settle into her home, the new Geraldine, a four-year-old milker, had a goatling (a female aged between 12 months and two years) called Jet to keep her company. On arrival, the pair were like children in a sweet shop, happily tucking into various leaves and shrubs around the garden. And Geraldine proved so compliant that she even won the heart of confirmed townie Giles.

'The goats are marvellous. I'm not really an animal person and wouldn't pretend to be, but the goats are lovely, like little warm hairy people. They're not butty and I took to them immediately. When I was a kid my parents had a place in the New Forest, but I never really cracked the countryside because I was scared of cows and ponies. The New Forest is full of them. I would set off for a walk, come out of the front gate, see a cow then go back home and watch TV. I'm probably still a bit like that, but goats have genuine charm – I think I may have found my mammal.'

Goat Notes

In his *Complete Book of Self-Sufficiency*, John Seymour wrote: 'For the self-supporting smallholder the goat can quite easily be the perfect dairy animal. For the person with only a garden the goat may be the only possible dairy animal.'

But expert Brian Rhodes, who reared Geraldine and Jet, warns that keeping goats is not an easy option.

'First of all you have to have commitment, because it's a seven day a week job. It's the same Christmas Day as it is every other day. You still have to get up and feed them, milk them and look after them. Their feet have to be cleaned every six weeks and you have to keep on top of everything.'

Brian began keeping goats in 1970 when his doctor suggested switching to goats' milk to cure his psoriasis.

'You couldn't buy goats' milk then so I bought a goat!' he laughs. 'Then I got a book from the library, which said you shouldn't keep one goat on its own, so I bought another goat. Before I knew it I had 30 goats in the garden of our terraced house, and at one stage we had 120.'

Choosing a goat

For garden livestock a good milking breed is essential. Geraldine is a British Alpine, a favourite with smallholders in the seventies because of its high milk yield. Other popular breeds include the Toggenburg, the high yielding Saanen and the Anglo-Nubian, which provides richer milk in lower quantities.

'Normally you start off with a kid and a goatling,' advises Brian. 'That gets you used to keeping goats and they get used to you before they kid. If you start with a milker and you're not very good at milking, you'll upset her.'

Registering

Like the pig, the goat needs to have a County Parish Holding (CPH) number, which

LEFT TO RIGHT: Toggenburg, Saanen and Anglo-Nubian goat breeds.

could use as a step up to the foliage above, and an outer layer of wire mesh. Their shelter, to keep them out of the sun and rain during the day, was a simple, open-fronted shack constructed from untreated wood. Baskets of hay were hung at the side of the pen for the animals to graze on. A shed at the end of the garden was also cleared out so that they would have somewhere warm and dry to sleep at night.

While you may associate goats with mountains and wild terrains, they are not a winter-hardy beast and dislike being wet. A shelter in the pen is essential to keep off both sun and rain, as well as a dry, draught-free shed for them to sleep in at night. If there is a draught at ground level a low table or cot for them to sleep on is a good idea.

can be obtained from the Rural Payments Agency. (See page 220). Each individual goat must also be given two ear tags, or an ear tag and a tattoo, bearing its 12-digit herd number as issued by Defra's Animal Health Divisional Offices.

You must also fill in a Movement Record Book, detailing all visits off the premises, including trips to the vet. An Animal Transport Certificate is necessary if the goat is to be taken and left at another holding, including for shows. Records of vaccinations and medical treatments must also be kept.

Space and housing

Goats love to graze so the bigger the area they can access, the better. Recommended minimum outdoor space varies with the different breeds, but an average of at least 2.5m² (8ft²) per goat is a good guide.

They can also leap surprisingly high so the fences need to be at least 1.2–1.5m and made of strong wire mesh with firm posts. Giles and Sue's goat pen was the largest of the three animal enclosures. It had a wooden fence with horizontal bars, which the goats

Feeding

As with the other animals, kitchen scraps are no longer acceptable, but the wide variety of vegetation that a goat eats means they needn't be too costly to feed.

'It's probably cheaper to keep a goat than it is to keep a dog,' Brian explains. 'I go out and collect branches from the side of the road, and they eat a lot of that. Then they have hay, haylage (grass cut earlier than hay) and concentrate feeds.' Having said that, the quality of the milk depends on the quality of the food and 'if you want the best out you've got to put the best in'.

Grass clippings, silage and roughage from the vegetable patch are great, but a concentrated food may also need to be fed to them when they are milking. Plenty of fresh water should be available at all times.

Although they will happily munch her way through most trees and bushes in the garden, there are many plants, such as rhododendron, yew, laurel and bracken, that are poisonous to a goat.

Pig Tales

While goat fences need to be high to stop them from jumping over, the pigs present the opposite problem. When fencing off the pig pen, the chicken wire had to be dug deep down into the grass because they are notoriously good at digging their way out. In fact, in the 'Pig's Lib' episode of *The Good Life*, Tom and Barbara's new pets dug under the fence into Margo and Jerry's garden, leaving green-fingered Margo in a state of shock. And she was none too impressed when Barbara came begging for kitchen scraps, uttering the immortal line, 'I don't have food scraps – I have a waste disposal unit!'

As well as having an area of grass to dig up and roll around in, the pigs were provided with a fairy-tale home – of sorts. Just like *The Three Little Pigs*, they lived in a straw hut, which was typical housing for pigs in the self-sufficiency boom of the seventies because it was cheap to construct. The house was made out of straw bales, with planks on top. It could be moved around when the pigs had turned over a section of grass. Luckily, there have been no sightings of big bad wolves in the area.

Unlike Margo and Jerry, Giles and Sue couldn't have been happier about the arrival of Pinky and Perky, the ten-week-old

 'In the seventies Tom and Barbara really opted out of the system and it was probably a bit easier to slip off the radar then. Now you have to register with Defra, and the animal movement laws meant our pigs had to be moved to a special site for three weeks before they came here, so it's far more regulated. If they made *The Good Life* now, there would be endless scenes about the red tape. You'd constantly be having Defra inspectors showing up and Tom and Barbara trying to pretend that the leftover pork pies in the pigs' trough were in fact cabbages.'

Gloucestershire Old Spots, although they soon discovered they were far from house pigs.

'My top tip for pigs is don't bring them through the house, because they have no manners and they are obviously not carpet trained,' explained Sue. 'The first thing they did on arriving was void their bowels – both liquid and solid matter was deposited all over the hall!'

The pair were soon contented in their own strip of the garden, however, wasting no time in digging up the previously perfect grass and cosying up in their straw shelter.

'They are sweet,' Sue continued. 'The noise they make when they're stressed gives you tinnitus, but they are really nicely settled in now and it's a joy to see. They were sleeping in spoons earlier. They are gorgeous and they are rooting around, tilling the soil for us. Giles has brought the ketchup, ready for the bacon sandwich, which he feels he will inevitably be making.'

Due to changes in the law brought about by outbreaks of foot-and-mouth disease, BSE and bluetongue, each pig now comes with a great deal of paperwork and a whole new set of rules about movement and feeding. With kitchen scraps and leftovers now banned, Giles pointed out that things have dramatically changed since Tom and Barbara's day.

'My pig husbandry is mainly centred around hours of petting and belly stroking. These pigs are probably the most massaged pigs in the UK. You don't have to go the whole hog with the sort of spa care I give them; but do play with them as they're intelligent creatures that need stimulation.'

'There's an element of pointlessness in pig rearing in a modern age, compared to the seventies. Pigs are no longer dustbins, which is what they were in *The Good Life*, eating whatever leftovers are available. They used to cost nothing to rear, but now you have to buy pig pellets. You can feed them on garden waste like weeds, grass, fruit and cabbage leaves, but nothing that has been in the kitchen.

'It's a bit of a shocker when you read the new Defra regulations. No disrespect to the farmers who were obviously out of pocket and devastated by foot-and-mouth disease, but it makes the prospect of a pig for a smallholder increasingly unviable.'

GETTING PRACTICAL

Picking Your Pig

In the 1970s, self-sufficiency guru John Seymour expounded the art of the 'pig bucket'. This was kept under the kitchen sink and used to collect 'all the household scraps except such as are earmarked for the cats and dogs'. This practice is now illegal as pigs must not be fed leftovers, making the keeping of pigs a far dearer prospect than it would have been for Tom and Barbara Good.

Even so, pigs are fairly undemanding creatures and, as well as providing a great deal of meat after six or seven months of care, they will churn up your garden more efficiently than a Rotovator, manure the whole patch and leave you with perfect soil for planting.

Choosing the pigs

To protect and preserve the traditional breeds, and for good-quality meat, a pedigree line is strongly recommended. Pinky and Perky are Gloucestershire Old Spots, a hardy breed that traditionally live all year in the orchards of Britain, effectively clearing up the windfall apples. Other popular breeds include the Welsh, the Wessex Saddleback, Tamworth, Berkshire and British Lop.

Viki Mills, Vice President of the British Pig Association (BPA), points out that the correct paperwork is vital in supporting old breeds. 'The pig should be birth notified and correctly marked. There are legal markings required by

**CLOCKWISE FROM TOP LEFT:
Welsh, Wessex Saddleback,
Tamworth, Berkshire and
British Lop pig breeds.**

Defra to trace pigs back to holdings but the pedigree mark is essential for registration in the herd book. You are not supporting conservation unless the pig can be traced and have a pedigree. If the litter has been registered with the BPA it should have a tattoo, an ear notch or a tag. Contact the BPA for further advice, see Useful Resources page 220.

Space

Two pigs can live in a relatively small area, but the space needed depends on the breed and whether you intend to breed or simply rear a pig to 'finishing weight', i.e. for the freezer. The RSPCA recommend a minimum of 36m² (400ft²) per pig, and it helps if you have enough space to move the animal pens when they have successfully churned up the garden.

Pigs suffer from sunburn in hot weather, so a shelter is needed. Strong straw bales with a corrugated iron roof, a timber A-frame design or a corrugated iron shelter will do.

A healthy choice

A pig should not be purchased before it is eight weeks old, as a traditional breeder will not wean them before then.

If it is going to be a breeding pig you need to check that it has at least 12 or 14 sound teats that are well spaced. It's not always easy to tell a sound pig at a young age, but any animal over three weeks old should have visible underlines if the teats have not already appeared. If you are just buying for meat, you still want them to be healthy, so don't buy undernourished runty-looking pigs. Buying privately from a breeder is better than buying them from a market.

Feeding

Some bought food will be necessary, but you can supplement the pigs' diet through your own vegetable garden by growing extra potatoes, beetroots or turnips and

by feeding them fallen fruit. Pigs also need milk by-products. Defra guidelines state that 'liquid milk or colostrum may be fed to pigs kept on the same holding as that on which the milk or colostrum originated'. So the goat could come in handy.

Registering and movement

As with a goat, a pig requires a County Parish Holding number (CPH) from the Rural Payments Agency. Their transit must be accompanied by an AMLS2 document, provided by the seller, and you must send the white copy to your local Trading Standards Animal Health Department within three days of the pigs arriving. They must then be registered with Defra within 30 days and a document with the CPH and herd numbers will be sent to you. Once on your property, the pigs must not be moved again for 20 days and subsequent movements must be logged in a movement book.

PART TWO
FOOD
FOR
FREE

BREAD AND CHEESE 4

For Tom and Barbara, the foray into self-sufficiency meant that anything that could be produced at home was off the shopping list. As well as fruit, vegetables and eggs, there was livestock for meat and, of course, Geraldine – referred to by Tom as 'a rhinoceros in goat's clothing' – for dairy produce.

The Goods' goat provided milk for their tea, cheese and butter, but it took the couple a while to master. Tom picked up an old wooden churn and, after hours of turning, ended up shaking the contraption in a desperate attempt for results. The glut of milk also provided Barbara with a few extras because, as she confided to Margo, 'a pint of goat's milk equals two pairs of knickers'.

And to go with the home-produced cheese Barbara had to tackle the old stove and bake her own bread – again with initially disastrous result.

Today, with the rise in foreign travel and increased culinary knowledge, goat's cheese has become commonplace. Forty years ago, however, it was a strange delicacy, only eaten in Europe and beyond and rarely seen on sale in the UK. To a nation brought up on cow's milk, goat's milk was virtually unheard of for human consumption.

In recent years many people have switched to goat's milk for health reasons. It is more suitable for those with lactose intolerance and can help clear up skin complaints such as eczema and psoriasis. It is closer in make-up to human milk, making it easier for people to digest.

Equally, a backlash against the mass-produced, preservative-packed loaf has led to many families trying out long-forgotten baking skills – and the result has an added green aspect. Add some pure goat's cheese to homemade bread and perhaps some homegrown tomatoes and you have the perfect organic, eco-friendly lunch. Not only do you have the benefit of knowing that your food is free from damaging additives and preservatives, but your carbon footprint is shrinking with all the food miles you have saved.

For Giles and Sue, both novices in the arts of milking and bread baking, the challenge was to produce their own meal, from udder to table. Enter one very placid goat and one very bossy celebrity chef.

Wholemeal Bread Flour

1.5 kg 3.31 lb

(Don't) Pull the Udder One

Before Giles and Sue could taste the delights of fresh goat's cheese, they had to face one of their most daunting challenges – milking. For this, they required a milking stand, some food, a bucket and one extremely patient goat.

Luckily Geraldine, who was coming towards the end of her milking cycle, was happy to oblige, even quite late in the afternoon when milking was long overdue. 'Normally goats are milked first thing in the morning and then again at night,' explained Brian Rhodes. 'If they'd have had one of the other goats, they wouldn't have got near her at this time of day because her udder would be hard and sore.'

The unsuspecting milker, or nanny goat as she would previously have been known, was led onto a wooden stand, which Sue referred to as 'the stocks'. A bucket of feed was hung on a rail at one end and Geraldine duly tucked in as Giles and Sue went in to try their hand at the udder end.

'She only has two nipples,' observed Giles. 'Is that normal?'

'I only have two nipples,' Sue shot back. 'Is that normal?'

After wiping the udder with a clean, warm, damp cloth, the amateur milkers got to grips with the teats and began to fill the bucket with fresh goat's milk, albeit relatively slowly.

'I really enjoyed milking. It's amazing to get fresh foaming milk, unpasteurized, with none of this government red tape and homogenized nonsense. I don't normally like goat's milk, but I could drink the whole bucket. It's delicious. I thought that the teat would be hard and rubbery, but it's actually pretty soft. Our milking was very slow, though. If you see an expert milking it's "yank, yank" and you have a bucket in a nanosecond. Giles and I managed about 2cm in what seemed like an hour.'

'I went to milk a horse once on another TV show. I went all the way to Belgium and I couldn't bring myself to do it. A horse is such a big thing with a black leathery udder, which is really hot and hanging underneath a pooey smelly leg/armpit. It didn't really appeal to me. But I like Geraldine – she's warm and smells of babies – so this was much easier.'

'Forget Scrabble, this is now my favourite thing!' exclaimed Sue. 'This is strangely satisfying.'

After several minutes of milking, the presenters' mischievous natures took over and they began to squirt warm, fresh milk at each other. However, Geraldine taught them a valuable lesson when she kicked the bucket over, spilling all the milk.

'I think the goat got a bit fed up with us mucking around and that's why she kicked it,' said Giles.

'If my head was in the stocks and people were pulling my udders tentatively, I'd probably do the same thing,' joked Sue. Luckily Brian's granddaughter Jade, who was taught to milk before she could walk, finished the job in expert style, filling the bucket in a fraction of the time it had taken Giles and Sue to fill just half.

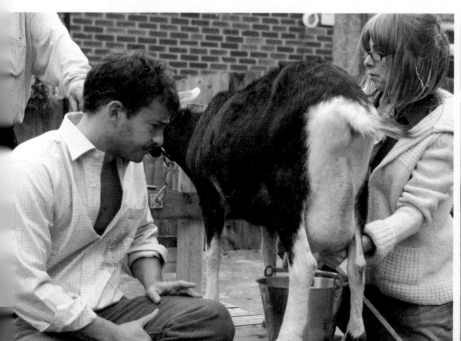

Tips on Milking

A milking stand with a stanchion to secure the goat's head is useful, but not essential, according to Brian. 'We used a milking stand, but you don't necessarily need one,' he explains. 'Walk up to the goat and start milking and she'll stand still.'

Before starting, wipe the goat's udder with a clean, warm, damp cloth, which will trigger milk letdown as well as washing the udder. Then wrap your thumb and forefinger round the base of the teat and squeeze with the middle finger.

'Squeeze don't pull,' Brian emphasizes. 'You're not a bell-ringer. Gently squeeze alternate teats. Practise makes perfect with milking and the more you do it, the better you get.'

Maintain a tight grip with the thumb and finger to stop milk going back up the teat and make sure you spray the first squirt of milk away from the bucket as this may contain some dirt and bacteria. As the goat nears the end of the milk and her teats go flacid, massage her udder to release the final few squirts.

The Good Life Gets Cheesy

Back in the seventies, goat's cheese was rarely seen on shop shelves or restaurant menus. In the absence of a cow, however, the Goods relied on Geraldine, 'the goat with the golden boobs', and Barbara's own endeavours, which ruined a fair few of her good tights in the straining process. The resulting culinary delight, served at dinner parties in their home, would have meant many of her neighbours tasting goat's cheese for the first time.

For the self-sufficient smallholder, goat's cheese is the perfect free alternative to the pasteurized cheese sold in supermarkets. But as Tom pointed out when Barbara made two whole 'legfuls' in 'Pig's Lib', the cheese doesn't keep very long so it's easy to make more than you can eat, and the problems come if you try and sell it on. Today, the EU's rules and regulations governing food safety make it virtually impossible for micro-businesses to sell unpasteurized cheese. The equipment and testing needed to pass products for public consumption are so costly that many smaller concerns have stopped making speciality cheeses altogether. But, after spending an afternoon making the soft cheese, Sue was surprised at how easy it was, and how tasty the results were, even if Giles wasn't so sure.

'The cheese we made was a first effort by a couple of urban losers. You couldn't compare what we made with something in a supermarket – they wouldn't sell it. Our cheese reminded me of when I was at boarding school and we were very short of food, so we'd eat practically anything. We would get a pint of milk every day and, in the summer, if you didn't get round to drinking it, it would have separated three days later. So you pour off the little bit of liquid and you're left with cheese, which you could only get out by smashing the top off the bottle and eating with a spoon. It usually had bits of glass in it, which slightly undermined the texture.'

'We took a bucket of fresh goat's milk, put it on the stove, boiled it, added three tablespoons of lemon juice so it curdled, cooled it down, drained it in a pair of tights and we ended up with a soft ball of very mild goat ricotta. I thought it was delicious. I don't normally like goat's cheese, but I loved our goat's cheese.'

HOW TO MAKE GOAT'S CHEESE

2 litres (4 pints) goat milk
Juice 2 lemons
Cheesecloth or a clean pair of old tights

1. Heat the fresh milk in a large pan. Once it starts to simmer add the juice of two lemons and simmer gently until it starts to separate, stirring constantly.

2. Take it off the heat and continue to stir until the milk is separated into curds and whey.

3. When it has cooled, drain it through cheesecloth – or simply pour the mixture into the leg of a clean pair of tights, à la Barbara.

4. Allow the whey to drain off, either by stirring or by squeezing the curds to get out more moisture.

5. String up the tights/cheesecloth over the sink or across an upturned chair with a bowl underneath it to collect moisture and allow it to drain for a few hours.

6. You now have soft cheese – this is tasteless without flavouring so you can add a little salt (which acts as a preservative), some herbs, garlic or chives.

The Bread of Life

Who can forget Barbara Good's first attempt at baking bread? The loaf that emerged from the wood-burning stove in 'The Thing In The Cellar' was roughly the size of small shed. With falling bread prices after the seventies, home baking became less fashionable, but today, with the invention of breadmakers and increased consumer concern over additives and preservatives in food, baking is back. For Giles and Sue, however, attempting to create the perfect loaf in a solid fuel stove was an entirely new experience.

Luckily celebrity chef Rosemary Shrager was on hand to help out. The formidable star of *School for Cooks* had a Rayburn of her own in the sixties and seventies and knows their pitfalls only too well. The trickiest part is maintaining the correct temperature and, unlike Giles and Sue, who were banned from burning wood due to changes in the law, Rosemary found a mixture of coal and wood was the most effective. She used coal to smoulder overnight and keep the fire alight, while wood could be piled in to raise the temperature when necessary during the day.

These problems came flooding back during the bread-making session at the Good Life house.

'One of the hardest things is trying to keep the heat level,' she recalled. 'That was really difficult because it can go up and up and then down and down. With Giles and Sue's range I was trying to control the temperature, but I'm sure I got the whole thing the wrong way round. I used to cook with one of these, but every stove is different and you have to learn how to cook with each one.

'The temperature is always hotter at the top than at the bottom, obviously, so we had to put one of the loaves back because it wasn't cooked enough. The other one was just perfect. The Rayburn bakes the most gorgeous bread but, to be honest, it's extremely difficult.'

Giles was delighted that the more successful of the two loaves was his, and he found the end result well worth the effort. 'The bread making went very well. It was easier than I thought,' he said. 'It was a little bit tricky in the Rayburn and even the better of the two loaves – which was mine – was nice and crusty on the top but a bit soggy underneath. It was lovely dense meaty bread, but God it would make you fat!'

'There is something better than Giles's bread making and that's his ability to remain modest in the face of victory,' retorted Sue. 'Actually, his bread *was* better. You know how an animal before slaughter becomes stressed and tense – that's what happened to me under the pressure of Rosemary shouting at me. My bread shrunk like a testicle in the Arctic.'

The Perfect Loaf

Imagine the smell of freshly baked bread wafting through your house and tickling the tastebuds. Sliced loaves may be cheap, but their taste isn't a patch on the real thing. Rosemary is adamant that we should all get back to the art of baking.

'Bread is incredibly simple to do, and it's jolly good exercise. Kneading the dough is a bit of a workout.' she insists. 'Today's bread is so awful; I call it "Bread Botox" because it's full of water, enzymes and horrible things they don't tell us about. Baking your own bread is incredibly important for your health, but it's also fun to do with the family.

'You can start off with a really good basic loaf and then you can add your own flavours to it. It's wonderful. Have fun. Don't be scared.'

But don't be tempted to rush out and buy an expensive breadmaker – Rosemary has little time for these modern gadgets.

'They make cotton wool. As far as I'm concerned that's not bread. How can it be kneaded, how can you tear the gluten? You've got to work it yourself, get your hands in there.'
The TV cook has an important tip for getting your dough to rise – don't let the dough get too warm as temperatures above 50°C (122°F) will kill the yeast. And should you be working on a similar stove to Giles and Sue, Rosemary has one final piece of advice: 'Start high and keep an eye on it,' she laughs. 'Then just wing it! That's all you can do.'

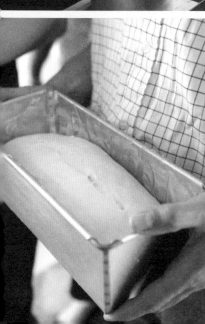

'I have quite a healthy diet, so I try to avoid eating lots of stodge. That loaf must have 6,000 calories in it – it was like a cake – but it was so nice. If you got a big slice of that every morning with your bacon and eggs you'd be the size of a house.'

ROSEMARY SHRAGER'S WHITE LOAF

750g (1¾lbs) strong plain flour
50g (2oz) cold butter, diced
25g (1oz) fresh yeast
550ml (17fl oz) water
15g (½ oz) salt

1. Grease the tin well.

2. Put the flour into a large bowl and rub in the cold butter. Add the yeast and mix well, then add the water and mix until it forms a dough.

3. Knead it on a work surface for about ten minutes. Add the salt and knead for a further five minutes.

4. Put the dough into a bowl, cover it with lightly oiled cling film, and leave to rise until it has doubled in volume.

5. Knock back (knead again) and put the dough into the prepared tin.

6. Leave to rise again for about 45 minutes. While the bread is rising, heat the oven to 220°C/430°F/Gas 7.

7. Put the dough into the oven. After 20 minutes, reduce the heat to 150°C/300°F/Gas 2 and cook for a further 25 minutes.

8. Remove the bread from the oven and tap on the bottom. If it sounds hollow it is ready.

THE CHICKEN OR THE EGG ✿ 5

In the classic episode 'Say Little Hen', a patronizing invitation to share Margo's 'canard à la paysanne' drove Tom to suggest slaughtering a chicken – just six hours after their arrival. After accusing their neighbours of declaring a 'war on want', Tom fumed, 'As a matter of fact we've got something a bit special laid on in the food line ourselves – and it will all be home grown and delicious.'

Tom practised strangling the bird using a bag of onions, then demonstrated with a chopper, before pulling an air pistol out of the kitchen drawer, marching to the chicken shed and telling the hapless bird to close her eyes as he took aim.

Finally, the Goods sat down to a candlelit dinner and the lid of the silver platter was raised with a flourish to reveal one poached egg. 'How can you miss a chicken from six inches?' asked Barbara, to which Tom retorted, 'It ducked!'.

Of course, Tom did eventually get used to the idea of slaughtering his chickens for the Sunday roast, but vegetarian Sue was not as keen for Giles to conquer his squeamishness to the same end. And although Giles is a confirmed meat lover, he was not quite ready to despatch a valuable member of the flock.

'At the moment they are laying eggs so it wouldn't be economically viable to put them on the table,' he said. 'But as soon as they stop laying, I would happily take off their heads with an axe and make a slow-cooked *coq au vin* out of them.' However, he later admitted he might actually be unable to carry out the final act himself.

'The first egg was brilliant, so exciting. All you have to do is buy the chickens, give them a home and – pow – there's an egg. That was a great moment. If Sue had her way, the chickens would die of old age and be buried with full military honours. I think they ought to be killed when they stop providing eggs. Although, for all my bloody-fanged carnivorousness, I'm too squeamish even to pick them up, so when the time comes we'll have to call Fred Hams in to finish them off.'

'I immediately wanted to cook the first egg. You get a smallholding and the next morning you can have an egg for breakfast, which I loved. Although, if you're Giles, you would also want to carve off a bit of the pig for bacon.'

From Coop to Kitchen

In the seventies Tom would have been perfectly within his rights to slaughter his own chickens and in that sense nothing has changed. While there are strict laws about the slaughtering of livestock, they don't apply to poultry when it comes to the smallholder. As they provide eggs as well as meat, chickens are one of the most economical and environmentally friendly creatures to rear.

'Poultry is the one thing that you can kill on the farm and sell from the farm gate,' explains turkey farmer Paul Kelly. 'You can't do that with any other species. So there's no food miles involved at all.'

Defra rules for commercial slaughtering of poultry state that 'a bird must only be stunned, slaughtered or killed in a slaughterhouse by someone who is aged 18 or over and who is licensed'.

However, no licence is required for slaughtering a bird by 'dislocation of the neck or decapitation as a means of routine killing in a non-approved premises situated on the farm where the bird was reared', providing the bird is slaughtered for private consumption. There is also no licence required to sell 'small quantities' of poultry meat, slaughtered on the premises, to a local retailer, although a record must be kept for each sale. See Defra's website (page 220) for further guidelines on poultry slaughtering.

The Art of Bartering

With 12 chickens, each laying up to seven eggs a week, any self-sufficient couple will soon have more eggs than they can eat. For Tom and Barbara, this, along with surplus vegetables and goat cheese, provided their income.

But it wasn't just money they got for their eggs. Tom used them for bartering, swapping two for a copy of *Pig Breeder's Weekly* at his local newsagent. Barbara's bartering skills were not so good. After telling the window cleaner they could 'work something out', he got the wrong end of the stick and thought she was offering a bit more than a couple of eggs. When he found out the truth, he was so embarrassed he cleaned the windows for free!

At the twenty-first century *Good Life* house, the chickens soon settled into laying and popping out enough eggs for breakfast, lunch and dinner on a regular basis, so Giles decided to try bartering himself. While Sue wisely steered clear of lecherous window cleaners, Giles set off to a local butcher armed with a large box of freshly laid produce. He took in 14 eggs and came out with eight rashers of bacon in return. 'The butcher said that people go into his shop quite often to try to barter. He often gets offered goat, but he can't sell the meat.'

How to Pickle Eggs

The pickled egg has long been a traditional snack in British pubs and a perennial favourite in fish and chip shops. In *The Complete Book of Self-Sufficiency*, John Seymour recommends pickling eggs in spiced vinegar to give them a little more flavour. You will need 1 litre (2 pints) of vinegar per dozen eggs. But be warned, the smell of eggs lingers for quite a while!

1. To sterilize the jars, place them in a large pan of water, bring to the boil and leave to cool.

2. Fill the sterilized jars with vinegar (wine, cider or malt).

3. Add spices to the vinegar, such as mace, allspice, cloves, peppercorns and mustard seeds.

4. Hard boil your eggs.

5. Shell the eggs then pack them in sterilized jars.

6. Cover with a little more vinegar and add a few chillies if desired.

7. Screw the lid tightly on the jar and leave for two weeks before eating.

THE GOURMET GOOD LIFE ❀ 6

With Tom dropping out from his well-paid job in the giveaway plastic toy industry, the Goods had to sacrifice some luxuries, which included the 20-year-old malt and fine wines they so enjoyed.

Occasionally they were able to indulge in Jerry's well-stocked liquor cabinet, but at home they were reduced to Tom's 'Pea Pod Burgundy'. At the grand opening of the first bottle, Barbara wrinkled her nose and declared, 'If that's the future, I'm going to kill myself.' But she soon developed a taste for it, polishing off a bottle with Margo after the pigs were taken away by the council.

In contrast, Margo and Jerry seemed to be constantly sipping gin and tonics on the patio, however early in the day. A creature of habit, Jerry's routine was to walk through the door, drop his briefcase and head straight for the drinks cabinet, while his bountiful lady reclined on her sun lounger with a cigarette in one hand and a cocktail glass in the other.

A Good Year

In the spirit of the original show, Giles and Sue decided to sample the best of both lifestyles, starting with making their own wine and cider. Organic gardener and broadcaster Bob Flowerdew, who called in to show Giles and Sue the wine-making ropes, grew up in a farming family and has years of homebrewing experience. He revealed that wine – especially the pea pod variety – was not the traditional beverage of those living off the land, for simple economic reasons.

'Most country people would not have made wine because you have to add so much sugar,' he explained. 'Certainly they wouldn't have done so before sugar became more affordable. You need about 2lbs of sugar to a gallon to make wine, 3lb if you want a strong wine. If you simmer pea pods you get very little sugar, so you are only using it for the flavouring. If you make wine from gooseberries, strawberries, plums and, of course, grapes, they carry some juice, which contains sugar. Even then, most of them wouldn't make a wine that was strong enough to keep without adding more sugar.'

Despite growing grapes in his garden in Norfolk, Bob has now stopped making his own wine.

'I found that I was buying grape juice to drink and making a mediocre wine from the grapes I grew. Then I realized I could buy good organic wine and make my grape juice for free. It was an upgrade on both sides.'

Although he doesn't making his own wine, Bob did manage to source some country wines, including apricot, cowslip, dandelion, gooseberry, nettle and parsnip, which he brought along to share with Giles and Sue.

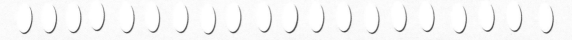

'The parsnip was sort of sweet and rooty, but the one that really took the enamel off my teeth was the gooseberry. I was left with brown stumps. It's not something you want to swill round your mouth, put it that way. We cleaned our drains very well with it afterwards.'

'The wine was a bit rubbish. But, the thing about homemade wine is that it does the trick. It gets you where you want to go, and if you've had a hard day of self-sufficient gardening you probably just want to get hammered, no matter what.'

Despite not being impressed by the homemade wines, after refusing to let Sophie Grigson have the pea pods for her pea and mint soup (see page 61), Giles was determined to try his hand at Tom Good's famous beverage. And while he is used to sipping the vintage stuff in Michelin-star restaurants, it's the first time he has actually attempted to produce it himself.

'I tried home-brewed beer when I was about 18,' he recalled. 'We all got really excited and went off to get the vats and the buckets and all the paraphernalia, but the sterilizing stage was so boring that by the time we'd done that, we couldn't be bothered to make the beer!'

As with all wine, patience is a virtue and the longer it's left the more drinkable it's likely to be – so Giles and Sue will have to wait to sample the 'Chateau Suburbia'.

GETTING PRACTICAL

Making Pea Pod Wine

In recent years, wine sales in the UK have soared and cut-price deals in the supermarkets means that most households can afford a glass or two with dinner. Back in the seventies, however, a bottle of imported wine was an expensive luxury and easy-to-use wine-making kits, often given as Christmas and birthday presents, fuelled a boom in home brewing.

As Bob Flowerdew recalled, there was a lot of help for first-time vintners. 'In the days of *The Good Life* they could have hired their equipment from a wine-making supplier,' he said. 'There aren't many hire places now, but there was a big home-brew trend in the sixties and seventies. I guess it was an economic measure as much as anything else. There were shops that sold big cans of juice to make your wine from, which was revolting. These places still exist, but there don't seem to be as many about as there used to be.'

Nowadays, as alcohol can be bought reasonably cheaply, it seems pointless to make your own for purely economic reasons. Carbon footprint concerns and a huge hike in quality has led to an upturn in sales of English wines in the last decade and there are now are over 400 commercial vineyards in England and Wales. But in the seventies,

self-sufficient families who fancied a local tipple were using elderberries, plums, dandelions and even potatoes to make wine, often following instructions from guru C.J.J. Berry, who published several books for the amateur throughout the sixties and seventies. As Jerry and Margo's faces testified when they bravely sampled the Goods' efforts, this was hard stuff indeed. Most homemade wines in the seventies had an average alcohol volume of 27 per cent compared to the 12–14 per cent typical of today's shop-bought varieties.

PEA POD WINE RECIPE

2.3kg (5lb) pea pods
1.4kg (3lb) sugar
1 tablespoon citric acid
½ teaspoon grape tannin
4.5 litres (1 gallon) water
1 teaspoon yeast

1. Wash the pea pods carefully and then boil them in the water until tender.

2. Strain and dissolve the sugar into the pod water.

3. Add the yeast and remaining ingredients, pour into a sterilized jar and seal with an air-lock.

4. Siphon off when wine begins to clear and bottle when fermentation has ceased.

How D'ya Like Them Apples?

With the British climate more suited to growing apples than wine grapes, it's not surprising that cider is a more traditional farmer's drink. For centuries the apple glut has been used to make scrumpy and cider, which was often shared out among the farmworkers at the end of a busy day picking fruit. In recent years, the traditional brews have given way to the factory-produced designer ciders, or 'white' ciders, made for the most part from imported apple concentrate. Sadly, as vineyard space in the UK increases, apple orchards are declining.

The joy of making cider is the simplicity of the recipe and the fact that it can be made from any apple. 'Like wine, some ciders are made with one variety of apple, but cider doesn't have to be,' explained Bob Flowerdew. 'But I'm not after a scrumpy or a strong psychedelic cider. I prefer something like an apple champagne.'

Before demonstrating the art of cider making to Giles and Sue, Bob treated them to his own range of tempting brews. 'I brought a 22-year-old one just to prove that it is still drinkable,' he said. 'It doesn't go off or become vinegary, it just becomes very sherry-like. Most wines are actually better with age, although cider doesn't age as well.'

After the unsuccessful wine tasting, Giles declared that the home-brewed cider was 'delicious' and Sue added that it 'was like rocket fuel, but lovely'.

Making Country Cider

Although Tom and Barbara concentrated on homemade wine, cider is a more economical option for the self-sufficient family. If there is room to plant a few apple trees, you have the main ingredient to hand. If not, a box of bruised fruits direct from a local orchard or farm shop would cost next to nothing when the apple season is underway.

'Two bucketsful would make a gallon, with no effort at all. Indeed, with some good apples, when you are doing it well and double pressing, you could get a gallon from one big bucket,' Bob explained.

'Half a teaspoonful of yeast and some sugary water will get it going if you've got a live yeast. It's always best to add a really strong fermenting mixture rather than dried, because you want it to go with a "woomf" rather than trickle away.'

Unlike wine, you won't have to wait a couple of years to sup the results. 'If you make it in the autumn, you can bottle it and drink it at Christmas. It's better the following spring and summer, but it is a relatively quick drink as opposed to most wines.'

And the outlay on equipment needn't be huge either.

'I prefer to make everything with bought-in equipment, a small press and crusher, but you don't have to,' said Bob. 'You can make cider very simply. You chop your apples, stick them in a pillowcase then put them in a very clean, strong plastic bag. Put a board on it and drive your car over it, then put it through a mangle or make a press by putting the crushed apple under a weight.'

The sugar content of your juice will determine how much alcohol is in your cider, so you may want to add more sugar later on in the process to make it stronger. Bob recommended a hydrometer to measure the potential potency.

'If you measure it with a hydrometer, as we did, you can tell how much sugar, thus how much potential alcohol is in it,' he advised. 'A cider will often be around 8 per cent or 9 per cent. If you want something a little more like wine, something a little stronger, then you need to add more sugar.

'The breakpoint is 1066 on the hydrometer. Water is essentially 1000 and as you add more sugar to it, it gets denser. So something that is 1010 or 1020 is very weak beer or shandy and above about 1080 it becomes undrinkable, it's potcheen, more for distilling than drinking. So the magic point is 1066 – before that it's beer and beyond that it's wine.'

BOB'S CIDER RECIPE

1. Wash the apples, cut them up and remove any bruising or maggots. 'You don't want any taint – you are trying to make something better, not worse, so scrupulous hygiene is essential.'

2. Put the cut-up apples through a crusher, which reduces it to small pulpous pieces.

3. Place immediately into a wooden slatted press and squeeze the juice into a demijohn. The pips and skin get caught in the slats so the juice comes through fairly clean.

4. Let it stand overnight and cool so that the remaining sediment can settle. In the morning it will be relatively clear.

5. Decant into another demijohn, add ½ teaspoon of live yeast to it, and ferment it for one to two months.

6. To make it stronger, wait until it has been fermenting for a few weeks, then add some sugar – about (113g) 4oz of sugar per 4 litres (1 gallon).

7. Decant off the dregs and let it stand a little longer.

BOB'S APPLE CHAMPAGNE

To make the clean sparkling cider that Bob specializes in, make the flat cider first then put it into pressure bottles with more sugar water.

'It's made very clean and when it's bottled just a little sugar water or honey is added to get the fizz,' revealed Bob. 'But you must be careful not to do that unless you have pressure bottles, otherwise you're making hand grenades. People do actually get seriously injured because they put the cider in to screwtop bottles while it is still fermenting. They are not intending to make sparkling cider, but it blows up. NEVER put homemade wine in screwtops, unless they are pressure bottles.

'In fact, the best things are clear plastic lemonade bottles. I wouldn't store it in them for any great length of time, but for convenience, if you are drinking it within a few months, they're easier to clean than glass and if you do get a secondary fermentation they won't kill you.'

Dining Out

Wining and dining is now an everyday occurrence but aficionados of *The Good Life* will remember that even the Leadbetters, the wealthier of the two couples, rarely went out for dinner. Jerry often ate at his golf club, but a restaurant meal was a truly special occasion.

Michelin-star chef Shaun Hill, who joined Giles and Sue for a seventies feast in London's retro restaurant Oslo Court, explained how the seventies revolutionized the cult of eating out.

'The 1970s was one of the most interesting periods for restaurant food because the availability changed dramatically over the decade,' he said. 'That's when we started to get strawberries out of season and all sorts of new foods air-freighted reasonably cheaply across the world. Changes in technology in food preparation were huge too. Food processors became available, which meant you no longer had to spend hours chopping vegetables, and people got wealthier so they could afford not to bother cooking if they didn't want to, except as a leisure pursuit.'

Restaurant culture was slow to catch on, but it was helped by cheaper chains, such as the Berni Inn steakhouses. 'The culture of eating out has come to British people quite late and it certainly wasn't part of their day-to-day life,' recalled Shaun. 'There were large changes in society that eating out then reflected – average, middle-class people started going abroad on holiday as they got a bit wealthier, and they began to feel confident about eating out in a recreational way.

'Berni Inns were a lot of people's introduction to eating out and feeling comfortable. Before, eating out meant you had to wear a tie and jacket; you felt an idiot if you didn't know what cutlery you should be using. A lot of the menus were in French and had dishes named after Napoleon's battles, so it felt like you'd entered the gastronomic freemasons and you didn't know the codes.'

Fellow diner and *Good Food Guide* editor Elizabeth Carter recalled that the Margos of this world were looking for a little 'je ne sais quoi' in their dining experience.

'The big thing was steak and the search for that little French restaurant that nobody else knew about – the snobby element.

Then there were the Italian trattorias where the waiters were terribly patronizing. The French and Italian restaurants were slightly up from the Berni Inns with their chequered tablecloths and candles.'

In our present-day Good Life experience, lunch for the time-travelling foursome consisted of grapefruit segments topped with sugar and grilled, served with a maraschino cherry, grilled sole in a lobster sauce and a choice from the ubiquitous and heavily laden dessert trolley.

'What we eat today is a lot lighter and fresher, with a lot more flavour,' said Elizabeth. 'In the seventies there was a lot of mucking about and a smothering of sauces, with cream and alcohol as the common ingredients – it was horribly fattening. When you look at recipes you wonder how anyone survived it.

'The big thing in the 1970s was chicken kiev. That started in the late sixties, but was so popular that in 1976 it was Marks and Spencer's first ever ready meal.'

Shaun spent the seventies 'wearing platform shoes' and working in the kitchens of Robert Carrier's Islington restaurant and then the Gay Hussar in trendy Soho. He explained why eating out locally would have been difficult for Margo and Jerry. 'There were very few restaurants in the suburbs,' he said. 'By the end of the seventies, restaurants had started to open in places like Dulwich and the movement was starting to gather pace. Nouvelle cuisine came in the late seventies and with it the cult of the chef as great artist.'

In terms of ethics, he believes there has been a huge leap in the attitudes of the diners. Instead of being delighted by out-of-season strawberries and the exotic taste of mango, many now want to know exactly where their food has come from and how far it has travelled.

'People care about the integrity of the ingredient as well as the skill of the people who have cooked it and that is a huge change since the seventies. There were no campaigns against factory farming, people didn't question where their food came from. That is a change for the good. Barbara and Tom were way ahead of their time.'

The Gourmet Good Life

121

Entertaining at Home

As dining out was so rare in the seventies, Sue and Giles decided to host their own dinner party à la Margo and Jerry. The lady of the house was often called upon to produce a sumptuous feast, often for the purposes of her husband's career advancement. 'Sir' was a frequent visitor to the Leadbetter household and even foisted visiting businessmen on them. In 'Mutiny', Jerry lost his job after refusing to accommodate a weekend visit as it clashed with Margo's production of *The Sound of Music*.

Sue's guests for dinner were TV critic Kathryn Flett and writer and historian Dominic Sandbrook, who sat down to a typical seventies meal of avocado mousse, duck à la campagne with boiled vegetables and oranges in Cointreau.

'The avocado mousse came in the shape of a fish, and we finished with a segmented orange,' laughed Sue. 'I put on a crap dinner party actually. Never serve segmented orange! The wheels of the hostess trolley got slightly mired in the tufted Wilton carpet so it was a tough push.

'The modern dinner party is much more casual. The seventies dinner party included more hanging around, and a big fanfare and fuss made of a woman's cooking after she'd spent hours in the kitchen.'

Another change in recent years is the reduction in the amount of smokers. In the seventies, as in *The Good Life*, people thought nothing of lighting up in each other's homes.

'I suspect people in the seventies were smoking in an effort to aid digestion of the overcooked duck and the booze-enrobed citrus fruit, which is never a happy combination,' joked Sue.

'The seventies booze at dinner was a slight improvement on the homemade wines, but it was still more nail polish remover than beverage. Unfortunately, I couldn't drink much, which is unlike me, because I felt this terrible weight of expectation. I had to go and get the trolley and present this meal with a great "ta-da" and in the end I just got tired.'

PART THREE
MANAGING
RESOURCES

ECO-TRANSPORT SOLUTIONS ✤ ⑦

Cars have become a modern-day essential, but there is no room for the usual modes of transport in a self-sufficient household: upkeep, tax, petrol costs and insurance would be difficult to afford.

Tom and Barbara used an old pram for transporting produce from the allotment to the house and begged the odd lift from kindly neighbour Jerry whenever necessary. But when the wheels finally fell off the wagon, Tom's bright idea was to turn the Rotovator, which was sitting idle in the garage, into a car.

'We'll be the envy of Surbiton, chugging between our allotments,' he boasted, even if it did only go at 7.5mph. He did concede, however, that they would need money for extra petrol, so the desperate couple were forced to take on the cleaning and gardening at the Leadbetters' house to pay for the vehicle.

Cheap Wheels

Taking a leaf out of the Goods' book, Giles and Sue turned their Rotavator into a makeshift vehicle that pulled a trailer and wooden bench. The resulting contraption was far from eco-friendly, unlikely to pass any MOT and would certainly be banned from the London Low Emission Zone. In terms of practicality, the experiment was a disaster.

'It worked up to a point, in that it went forward,' laughed Giles. 'You can't reverse so you have to pull it back, and driving it down to the end of the road probably emptied the petrol tank, so it's not the most fuel-efficient mode of transport. It weighs half a ton, about the same as a small modern car, and if you weren't paying attention you started drifting to one side.'

'And at one point it was heading towards a Porsche Cayenne,' Sue reminded him.

'The other thing is that I couldn't remember, from when I last used the Rotovator, how you stop it, because it doesn't have a brake,' added Giles. 'You stop it by depressing the clutch and putting it in neutral, which, in an emergency situation, is not all that satisfactory. It's a vintage model and it didn't have second gear, so we only had first and third.'

While Tom and Barbara may have been able to pootle along at 7mph on the relatively uncongested roads of seventies Surbiton, the 2010 model did less than 5mph and would be something of a liability on the busy streets of north London.

'We could have walked alongside it quicker,' said Sue. 'On reflection, having travelled on the park bench, which started to come loose as we drove, I'd be tempted to walk, or take a bus!'

'It was like a return to the golden age of motoring. I felt we should have had someone walking in front with a flag.'

WARNING
Beware of
rotating blades.
See there is no
one in direction
of driving.

GETTING PRACTICAL

Greener Travel

One of the biggest conflicts between the lifestyle of a smallholder and the desire to be green is the issue of transport. For most, a car, van or truck is necessary for moving produce and animals, but the most environmentally friendly models, such as hybrids, also tend to be the latest models and are therefore not cheap to buy. Despite discounts on car tax for greener cars, there are still considerable running costs involved.

Buying the latest hybrid on the market may be out of the question, but there are many ways in which everybody's journeys can become more eco-friendly and save money at the same time. Investigate biofuels, which can be used in cars with a 5 per cent mix with ordinary fuel. Biodiesel, made from waste cooking oil, can be used in this concentration in all diesel models; the same concentration of bioethanol, made from plants, can be used in petrol models. Cut down on car journeys by walking or getting public transport whenever possible, and if you need to get behind the wheel, follow these eco-driving tips from the Energy Saving Trust:

1. Shift to a higher gear as soon as possible.
Driving at lower engine speeds reduces fuel consumption.

2. Anticipate road conditions and drive more smoothly.
Rather than last-minute braking, decelerate smoothly by easing off on the throttle as early as possible. This allows the car to decelerate using engine braking. With the car in gear and the throttle released, a modern car uses virtually no fuel at all.

3. Maintain a steady speed in as high a gear as possible.
Driving at a steady speed requires little effort for the engine. Avoiding unnecessary acceleration and heavy braking helps to reduce your fuel consumption.

4. Drive a little slower.
For most cars, the most efficient speed is 45–50mph. The faster you go above this, the more fuel you will use. Driving at 50mph rather than 70mph reduces your fuel consumption by 10 per cent at a stroke.

5. Switch off if you're stationary.
When stuck in traffic or waiting for someone, switch off your engine.

6. Keep your tyres properly inflated.
Under-inflated tyres cause excessive drag and resistance, increasing fuel consumption. Both over- and under-inflated tyres can be dangerous, so make sure your tyres are at their recommended pressure.

7. Switch off air conditioning.
Your engine has to work harder to power the air-conditioning. If you are driving at a low speed, open the window instead.

8. Close your windows if you are travelling at 50mph or more.
The aerodynamic drag on your car of an open window at speeds of 50mph or more adds to your fuel usage. Keep your windows closed at high speeds.

9. Remove roof boxes and racks if they are not being used.
A roof box or rack increases drag on your car, making your engine work harder.

10. Remove unnecessary items.
Carrying excess weight in a vehicle increases fuel consumption. Heavy or large items, such as tool kits and golf clubs, should be removed when not required.

'We sat behind the Rotovator while it gushed petrol fumes into our faces so, environmentally, it was quite poor. But it was fun to drive. You know when people say, "You really feel like you're driving this vehicle," that was very true of this. We actually had to get out and manually turn it.'

COMING OFF THE GRID

8

Tom's ingenious answer to reducing the electricity bills was an 'effluent digester', which he powered with dung from the pigs: 'Waste not, want not, pick it up and stoke it,' he cheerfully explained. They cut down drastically on their electricity use, but keeping the freezer going was essential to store the meat when the pigs were finally slaughtered, Tom explained.

   'Isn't that a bit ungrateful when they help power the thing?' was Jerry's heartfelt response.

   The homemade generator had a few teething problems. It made the chair directly above it vibrate violently, giving Jerry a shock when he sat down. Then, while Tom and Barbara were out, the generator broke down – a disaster for all the freshly caught fish Tom and Barbara had just put in the freezer that morning. But when Tom went next door to see if they could put their fish in Margo and Jerry's freezer, Jerry refused, national power strikes meant they were without electricity too.

The Goods would not have been alone in seeking an alternative source of energy in the seventies. As the Leadbetters suffering a power cut in 'The Thing in the Cellar' illustrated, both householders and businesses were subjected to long power cuts. In a bid to limit fuel consumption, a three-day week was introduced and rolling blackouts occurred often in 1974. The fear of running out of coal, coupled with anxiety over nuclear war, meant that new ideas about power became popular. In *The Complete Book of Self-Sufficiency*, published in 1976, environmentalist John Seymour suggested a homemade method for solar heating, by running water through a radiator on your roof or threading a hosepipe through a collection of glass bottles. He also suggested a similar system to Tom's: 'If we can take the dung of animals or men, extract inflammable gas from it in quantities that make the effort worthwhile, and still have valuable manure left over to return to the land, we are doing very well.'

Scientist Dr Marty Jopson, however, dismisses 'The Thing In The Cellar' as 'a complete fantasy'.

'You could get a little energy, but it would be horribly inefficient,' he explains. 'It wouldn't be a bad idea if you had lots of livestock, and there are instructions on the Internet for making these things. On *The Good Life* they burn the methane to heat water, which turns a turbine. You could just use the methane to cook your dinner on, which would be viable, but making enough electricity from the dung of one goat and a couple of pigs would be impossible.'

Giles and Sue sensibly eschewed the poo in favour of a Pelton Wheel, which is a modern-day take on the old-fashioned water wheel. The small, wooden hub has 12 ladles attached to it that, when placed under a stream of water, turn the wheel. The kinetic energy produced is stored as electricity. Giles and Sue used the hosepipe for their water stream. In theory, the higher pressure of the water as it's pressed through and out of the hosepipe should produce more energy per cubic litre as it hits the wheel than a regular stream of water.

'Because the water hits the ladles as a high-pressure jet rather than a 'sploosh', it doesn't just bounce off' explains Marty. 'The old-fashioned water wheels rely on a sheer mass of water moving

Dr Marty Jopson shows Giles and Sue how to power the Pelton Wheel using water from a hosepipe.

the wheel. For Giles and Sue's wheel, they should require less water used under a greater pressure. It was all well and good when I made it, and in my workshop it was working beautifully, but on the programme it was less successful than I'd hoped because Giles and Sue had very poor water pressure!'

Giles and Sue also tried a variation of the Pelton Wheel that was powered by a bicycle, unfortunately with limited success: 'The bike-powered mechanism was working fairly well, except for the fact their bicycle was rubbish. I designed the contraption to fit my bike, but theirs didn't quite fit, so I had to do some last-minute bodging. Unfortunately the bike kept falling out of the back cradle.'

Renewable energy technology has come on leaps and bounds since the seventies, but with our increasing reliance on electrical gadgets, Marty believes that coming off the National Grid would be a tough task for the self-sufficient suburbanite.

Coming off the Grid

135

'The last place you would want to choose to start generating electricity is the middle of suburbia. It would be better to up sticks and go somewhere where you have a water source, a good place to put up a wind turbine or somewhere really sunny, so you could use a photovoltaic system to generate electricity straight from sunlight.'

For those who still want to do their bit to reduce electricity bills and save energy, it is now a lot easier than it was 40 years ago.

'In the seventies there wasn't very much available to the average householder, but nowadays there's a lot you can do if you really want to get into generation,' advises Marty. 'There are schemes that allow you to put solar panels on your roof, and some of them will cost you very little or nothing. The "feed-in tariffs" the government has at the moment means that the payback time is quite quick. Solar hot water is easily achievable if a house has a south-facing roof. You can also now buy wind turbines for about £1000 at the big DIY stores, but they are not ideal because most areas won't really have the constant wind required. You need to be on a hill without too many trees and houses around. On a plus, renewable power supplies are at least available and much easier to get hold of now.'

While technology to create energy has moved on, so too has the ability to conserve it and this is where the real battle can be fought.

'Coming off the Grid? Don't even go there. Giles pedalled for about an hour and we got enough power to operate a really pathetic little hair dryer for 0.6 seconds.'

'Before you start generating your own electricity you should question what you need electricity for and how little electricity you can get away with using. Technology has really changed because we have increased the efficiency of appliances. With a bit of know-how you can keep energy usage incredibly low, with low-energy lighting, lower energy refrigeration and so on. If you are going to live the Good Life, lighting and a freezer are the two most important things you will need to power. We now have low-energy light bulbs and A+ rated freezers, which we didn't have in the seventies.'

Sue agrees that generating electricity in north London may be a stumbling block in the Good Life scheme.

'You have to look at the bigger picture. Live with a bit of mixed energy, a bit of solar, a bit of wind turbine if you can, but for most people coming off the Grid is not practical. You need to start thinking about easier things like having rain butts to conserve water, switching lights off or making sure you swap your halogen bulbs to something more energy efficient. Everybody can make a difference within their own four walls. It was impossible for us to get off the Grid because we couldn't generate the electricity, but it's all a great idea. Making it work is phase two.'

Let There Be Light

Candlelight is a great way of cutting down on electricity – romantic couple Tom and Barbara frequently enjoyed candlelit meals together. They were also given candles by Margo when their electricity was cut off, only to smugly hand them back when Tom built his own generator.

The self-sufficient family doesn't have to keep bees in order to shine a light: candles can easily be made from animal fat. Beef and mutton are best, preferably from around the kidney and loin areas, but any type of firm animal fat will work. The rendered and purified fat is called 'tallow' and has been used to make cheap candles for centuries.

The disadvantage is the smell and the fact that it is smokier than today's mass-produced varieties – not a good idea to burn instead of a scented candle.

How To Make a Candle

1. Take around 4–5kg of beef fat and place it in a large pot.

2. Pour in just enough water to cover.

3. Bring the water to the boil and continue to boil until all the water has evaporated and the fat has melted down to liquid.

4. Pass the fat through a fine sieve several times to filter out impurities – pieces of gristle or leftover meat.

5. Make the wick by taking a length of cotton twine and dipping it in the liquid to soak it through. Remove and allow to dry.

6. Pour the tallow into moulds, either dipping in the wick or placing the wick in beforehand, depending on the shape of the mould.

7. Allow the mixture to set.

8. You can scent the tallow with herbs from the garden or other household products.

REAPING THE HARVEST

In an attempt to recruit some harvest help in the local pub, Tom boasted that after a few days work 'we'll have enough food to last a year'. But the smallest setback can mean total disaster and having failed to find willing helpers, in 'Backs Against the Wall', Tom put his back out leaving Barbara to harvest alone. The following night, a fierce storm ruined the animal pens and the couple woke to find the garden devastated, with the pigs and goat happily munching through the crop. Luckily, Margo and Jerry returned early from a disastrous African holiday, and, despite Jerry's broken foot, helped get the harvest in.

   But there was another hurdle – making money out of the glut. After assuming the excess could help pay the mounting bills, Tom got a swift reality check at a local restaurant where he found that he would be unable to deliver in the quantities required. Barbara tried setting up a stall outside the house, but only managed to sell 2lbs of carrots!

Later on in the series, they found better outlets for their produce and, in 'Weaver's Tale', he told Barbara, 'our soft fruit ship has come in to the tune of £195.' This may seem a piffling sum today, but in the 1970s, £195 went a long way. In fact, Barbara concluded that it would pay for a year's water rates, petrol, tax and insurance for the car and two new pairs of shoes, with £10 left over.

Today's reality is that there are some bills, such as Council Tax and water rates, that will always need to be paid, so self-sufficient couples still need to make at least a little money from their plot. But would Giles and Sue's vegetable plots, livestock and homemade produce be enough to turn a profit?

Getting a Buzz

Although beekeeping was never a part of the Goods' garden production, it is one of the few things a smallholder can do better in a suburban garden than on a rural farm. 'In the country you tend to have monocultures, so you have huge fields with one single crop,' explains Jo Telfer, education officer of Harrow Beekeepers Association. 'Hedgerows have been lost, and there are few flowers so it's harder to get a crop of honey. In suburbia, there are huge areas of park and gardens and everybody tries to grow different things, which means there's nearly always something available for bees to forage on, even in the autumn and early spring, which you might not get if you were in the country.'

The north London house was an ideal place for a hive, being surrounded by large gardens boasting riots of colourful flowers. However, the occupants, especially Giles, were perhaps not suited to this particular form of food production.

'Bees would be a very good thing to keep, but I don't like insects. And I don't have a sweet tooth. Sue has a sweet tooth; I like eating pork. The only thing I could use honey for is to make honey-roasted ham and Sue's not going to let that happen. Everyone was going crazy for the honey and the comb, and it is one of the world's great miracles, these wonderful hexagons of honey. It was also the first time I'd ever seen a queen bee, which was amazing, but I just don't think I would ever keep bees.

'In a world where you don't have much or any money, you have to go back to the pre-Elizabethan era when we didn't have sugar so we sweetened things with honey. Without an income, we would need honey to make mead, chutney and other things and bees would be essential.'

Sue was a little more enthusiastic about the insect invasion and only slightly scared by the prospect of a sting.
'The bees were very powerful. You hold up these frames and they are crawling with insects, thousands of them; the whole thing is humming with life. It reminds you who's boss really – and it wasn't me! I found the end product amazing, absolutely delicious.'

The number of honey bees in the UK has declined over the last few years for a variety of reasons. As well as the disappearance of wilderness lands and hedgerows, tidy gardens and areas concreted for cars have meant less foraging available for the bees. One of the biggest factors, however, is the varroa mite, which originated in the Far East and reached UK shores in 1992. The mite, which lives in the cell where baby bees are born, causes deformities, such as small wings, stunted growth and paralysis.

'A lot of people who had been keeping bees for a long time, and knew it was physically hard work, thought, I've lost my bees, I'm not going to start again,' recalls Jo Telfer. 'But then there are many like me who, having got this wretched mite, decided the bees needed our help more than ever. Sadly, it has wiped out all our field colonies. We managed to find medication that was suitable for treating the hives, but the mites then became resistant to that and in 2006 we realized the mites were no longer dying when treated. We now have a different medication and research groups are still looking to find better ways of removing the mite.'

In 2006/07 a new bee-related crisis was registered, known as CCD (Colony Collapse Disorder), where worker bees from a beehive abruptly disappear. Reasons for this are not yet fully understood, but have been attributed to causes as varied as GM (Genetically Modified) crops, alien invasions, insecticides, mobile phone radiation, bacterial infections and malnutrition.

'The outfit was sort of Apollo 13, a full, white, nuclear-hazard-type suit, like something out of a film. Despite that, Giles was still terrified and threatened to sue everybody if he was stung, which made me laugh because I'm not sure who you'd sue. The individual bee or the collective hive? In the end, we didn't get stung, so we were alright.'

Money from Honey

Beekeeping start-up costs are expensive, but once set up there is little further outlay. A nucleus, which consists of a queen and four to five frames of bees, will set you back around £150. You'll need a protective suit, which costs around £100, and a hive, which you can buy through a local association in flat pack form or make yourself. Then there are jars and, if you intend to sell the honey, labels that must follow strict guidelines. It's safer, although unsurprisingly dearer, to get them professionally printed.

'In each colony you have 11 frames, which are the wooden bits that hang inside. Eventually all 11 should be covered with bees and brood [eggs],' explains Jo. 'Then the bees find there is no room because the queen has filled all the brood boxes with eggs, which take six weeks to hatch, so they store the excess food over the brood box, which we call the super. We restrict the queen so she has to stay in the larger box and, because she can't get there, you don't have any eggs or babies to worry about, just honey.'

In the last couple of years, there has been a massive surge of interest in beekeeping and the British Beekeeping Association currently has a waiting list for its beginner courses. But Jo is anxious to point out that beekeeping is not something you can go into halfheartedly.

'You have to be conscientious. This is not a five-minute wonder. Bees need to be constantly cared for. You can't just stick them in the garden and go away. You need to keep an eye out for symptoms of mite and you need to constantly check them, even through the winter.

'Other things to consider are that you need to have very tolerant neighbours, because their garden will have more bees than normal.

'Bees need water so a fishpond or swimming pool nearby is good, but if you haven't got those you need to provide water. A bird bath is fine, but it needs to be constantly topped up in dry weather. Finally, you need a strong back, because there's quite a lot of very heavy lifting.'

'The proper equipment to make sure you're not stung costs hundreds of pounds, so you'd be better off buying a lifetime's supply of honey. If you're prepared to do it with just a little mask and a pair of gloves, which I am not, you'd be alright. You can have your homemade beekeeping kit, but I need a proper anthrax suit if I am going anywhere near those bees.'

A typical colony will yield around 18–27kg (40–60lbs) of honey. Prices at market range from £3 to £7 a pound, so you will begin to get your money back within the first yield. The wax can also be used to make polish, face and hand creams and candles. But Jo insists that it is not a reliable source of income for a smallholder. 'So many things can go wrong, even with the best will in the world,' she warns. 'The only way to make money out of it is to breed queens and sell colonies, which is what the commercial people do.'

Jo's final piece of advice for budding beekeepers is to seek out the experts: 'I would recommend that you join your local association and they will tell you exactly what beekeeping entails. That will link you to the British Beekeeping Association, where you can get your insurance, cheaper equipment and lots of advice.'

Going in for the Kill

Barbara and Tom's pigs, Pinky and Perky, enjoyed a happy life in their Surbiton garden, but there comes a time on every smallholding when the animals end up in the freezer. While one pig can yield a lot of meat, and will happily see a family through the winter, intensive farming has driven meat prices down in the last 30 years. Rare breeds, like the Gloucestershire Old Spot, are less commercially viable than those reared for supermarket shelves.

'The old-fashioned breeds have gone out of favour with supermarkets because all people want to buy is a chop,' explained Sue. 'So the supermarket pig has to basically look like an upright piano with a long, long back for lots of chops, and spindly legs because no one wants leg of pork any more.'

The cost of buying and feeding a pig until it is old enough to slaughter is around £180. To find out whether their porcine pair had literally eaten their profit, Sue and Giles called in master butcher Peter Gott, who also rears rare breed pigs on his Cumbrian farm.

He had some sound advice for our Good Lifers. 'Some abattoirs charge £40 to slaughter, although I only pay £15. You could also be charged £1 a kilo to cut it up, which means £70 for an average pig. When you factor in the food costs, there would be no money out of it whatsoever if you sell it as fresh pork.

'At supermarket prices you could get £250 for a pig or a farm shop would give you £350. But if you cure it, make some bacon and ham, you could get £500. Another problem with fresh pork is your window

'You would never make any money from farming just two pigs, but we went through all the different cuts and there's an awful lot of good eating on there for a small family. Not just the legs and belly and chops, but all the lovely innards: the kidney, liver, spleen, the trotters and snout and cheeks (so-called Bath chaps) and the tail, which crisps up lovely for salads. In the old days the inhabitants of a small hamlet would fatten a single pig together to help get everyone through the winter.'

of opportunity, which is seven to ten days, after which your pork goes off, or you have to put it in the freezer.

By curing it and processing it you have a 6–15 week window of opportunity and you have a value-added product. It's not that hard once you understand the basics. You add salt and sugar with nitrite to a product – you can do it in a polythene bag, in a bath or on a table – and you have nice tasty bacon.'

To maximize the flavour, Peter recommends a later slaughter. 'When a pig gets past 22–24 weeks old there is a pH change in the meat that makes it perfect for curing. The Italians and the Spanish don't cure a pig under nine months old, and it's the age that makes the flavour so exceptional.'

As there are strict laws about the transportation of animals for slaughter, Peter strongly advises that you check out your nearest suitable facility.

'In the last 25 years, we've lost nearly 1000 abattoirs, mainly because of EU regulations and bureaucracy. There are now only 350 slaughterhouses in the UK and some of those are tied to supermarkets or only slaughter one type of livestock. However, if you can find a local abattoir, put in a telephone call, book the pig in and, provided the distance is no further than 67.5km (42 miles), you can put it in a trailer and take it there.

'If you are driving beyond 67.5km (42 miles), you have to get an animal transportation licence, which means a day course, and that will set you back another £150.'

Committed carnivore Giles was keen on the idea of curing the meat. 'Peter told us we could make proper ham, like Parma ham, out of those legs, air-dried, and pancetta from the belly, which would be wonderful and very exciting.'

Even vegetarian animal lover Sue was impressed with the idea of rearing happy, rare breed pigs that would eventually become pork products.

'I don't eat pig, but Peter was effectively saying that you don't keep a pig for profit – you will break even and in return you will have the most amazing meat from animals you have reared yourself. You reap the benefits of what you put in, so if you treat the animals well you get better meat. It would be great to encourage people to have these old-fashioned pigs and rear them, look after them, and use all the cuts of meat that we've stopped eating.'

A Meagre Harvest

The first opportunity Giles and Sue had to display their wares came in early July at the annual Kent County Show in Detling. The agricultural show, which showcases produce and livestock from around the country, attracts over 100,000 visitors every year. In a bid to make a buck, our modern-day Good Lifers harvested a few vegetables, packed up some jars of green tomato chutney, pickled eggs, bottles of pea pod wine and even a few handmade wooden house signs with painted numbers, including one, produced by Sue, that read 'Beware of the Coren'.

With a poor harvest of produce from the garden, Giles and Sue were keen to find another way to bid for glory at the prestigious show. The answer came in the shape of Perky, the Gloucestershire Old Spot boar. The pig had already won high praise from butcher Peter Gott, who said his lineage was so pure that 'if that pig could talk he wouldn't be talking to the likes of me and you'. After receiving a letter from the British Pig Association confirming the boar as 'a particularly fine animal and a real credit to the breed,' Giles and Sue decided to take their porcine pal along for the ride and enter him into the Confirmation Class. It is here that young animals are judged for their potential and whether they are a good example of their breed.

Perky prepared for the rigorous contest by settling happily into a comfortable stall for a good long sleep, while Giles and Sue began their assault on the unsuspecting folk of Kent. They offered their potent pea pod concoction and a free pickled egg to anyone brave enough to try one. It wasn't long before they were in trouble with the authorities, however, having neglected to apply for a licence to sell alcohol. After a scolding from the official, the practical pair concluded that their 'try before you buy' policy would put off any potential wine customers, but might leave them tipsy enough to buy the chutney.

'It all went very well, considering the awfulness of the products,' said Giles. 'People tasted the wine and didn't even puke. It seems they'll drink anything in Kent. We sold quite a lot of chutney. There was no interest in the pickled eggs, which is hardly surprising – I tried one and it was truly rank.

'Bizarrely, there was also some interest in the house signs. Although, to my shame, I was unable to answer the technical questions such as "What kind of wood is it?"'

After a well-earned rest, Perky perked up for show time and Sue took him into the enclosure, watched by an eagle-eyed judge. As with all the pigs, Perky was led around the pen with a 61 x 61cm (2 x 2ft) board that controlled the direction he was walking in. But Sue had a special trick up her sleeve, having bought a pot of honey from a nearby stall and smeared it on the board to help lure Perky towards the smell. After a fine first outing, the promising pig walked away with a second place rosette in the Confirmation Class, having been narrowly beaten by a pair of Texel sheep.

Afterwards, Sue revealed the real reason for the lack of vegetables on the stall – and why Perky was in fine fettle. 'Before we came, the pig got out in the garden and it went into snowplough mode with its nostril. It tilted its head at 45 degrees, rootled through an entire patch in a nanosecond and, as quick as you could say "Not my beloved beetroot" the whole lot had gone. The canes got knocked down, ruining the French beans, and its trotters were running free form over the delicate salad leaves. But then it did win second best four-legged, big-bollocked mammal so that's good.

'I'm very happy and proud of him. It must have been all the vegetables he ate out of our patch.'

CLOCKWISE FROM TOP RIGHT: Giles and Sue settle Perky the boar in his pen at the Kent County Show. They also took a batch of green tomato chutney to sell, made with tomatoes from the garden.

Hedge Veg

After their initial failure to sell to restaurants, in 'Just My Bill', Barbara set up a stall outside their Surbiton home, but only managed to sell 2lbs of carrots before Jerry quickly pointed out that she was trading without a licence. Meanwhile, Tom is challenged by a greengrocer while wheeling cauliflowers and greens through the streets and runs home after he is threatened with a beating.

After being forced to sell to the restaurant at a loss, they are unable to pay their rates until they find enough coppers down the back of the sofa and change a 500 peseta note to make up the difference.

In order to make some money from the Good Life venture, Sue and Giles decided to rely on the integrity of their neighbours and set up an 'honesty table'. The stalls set outside houses in many rural areas to sell fruit, eggs and veg rely on passers by to contribute what they feel they should pay. They are particularly commonplace in the Channel Islands, where they are known as 'hedge veg'.

'It's a nice way of selling, and living in Cornwall, I'm used to seeing farms with makeshift shelving or a cart outside where you take the produce and just put money in,' said Sue. 'It was really nice to trust in those old-fashioned values.

'Rural communities are much more used to the notion that you stick stuff on a table and that's a valid way of buying things. There's a degree of suspicion in the urban or suburban community, where people grow up unnaturally close to one another, that anyone would be offering that kind of open-handed food retail policy. It's like, 'What's wrong with it?' It's all about changing people's attitudes actually and it's a really nice thing to do, especially if you're growing stuff and you have a glut. Better that than to see it rot.'

After deciding to grow organic vegetables on the family farm in Devon, in the mid 1980s, Guy Watson gave up his high-flying job as a management consultant and took it up full time. He started out with deliveries of veg boxes to locals and his company grew year by year until he began working with organic producers across the country to deliver local food elsewhere. Today, Riverford Organic Vegetables employs 260 staff, has 100 franchisees and makes 47,000 deliveries a week.

Casting an eye over the fruit and veg Sue and Giles had collected, Guy thought the pair had made a good start for amateurs.

'For a first attempt it wasn't bad,' he commented. 'Gardening and farming is extraordinarily difficult and you are not going to go in there with a shovel and be successful in your first year. There is a whole minefield of mistakes to be made and they've made a few of them. The potatoes were good, the cabbages grew well, but they'd neglected to harvest them at the right time so they all split. They grew marrows rather than courgettes, and no one wants a marrow, but some of the chillies and aubergines looked alright.'

In Barbara and Tom's shoes, however, Guy reckoned they would struggle to pay any bills on the proceeds of their glut.

'As a garden it was fine and you would have a few meals out of it but, as a commercial enterprise, it wasn't much good. They'd grown between £10 and £20 worth of vegetables, so I don't think it would help with the council tax much.'

While growing your own is to be 'wholeheartedly encouraged', Guy advised that selling your produce is no way to make money on such a small scale.

'We set up an honesty table and what we learnt was that some passers-by aren't very honest. There was a bit of pinching going on (allegedly!), although we did have one or two people who paid proper money for their organic veg. We got £2. It would have been enough in the 1970s to have bought us both a pint. Sadly, now, we could probably share a half.'

'To grow stuff commercially in a plot that big is completely ridiculous,' he said. 'If you are looking at it from a brutally commercial point of view you'd be better off not sowing the seeds in the first place. To harvest and sell them would take more time than it's worth and you could earn more doing a few hours on the minimum wage. That's not why people grow vegetables in gardens. Most people grow them because they taste better, they get satisfaction from doing it and they feel closer to what they produce, and those are very good reasons for gardening.

'This is not a way to beat the recession. You may have nicer tasting vegetables and will raise children with some connection to how food is produced and you may enjoy your food more and even be a little bit saner at the end of the day, but in terms of saving money it would be pretty piffling.'

In 'Just My Bill' Tom admits that his biggest mistake was growing common crops such as potatoes, cabbages and peas. After seeing the restaurant manager he tells Barbara, 'If you want to cash in on the sort of amounts we have, don't grow peasant foods.'

According to Guy, he has a valid point. 'The wholesale price for organic carrots is about £500 a ton, so a couple of kilos would sell for £1,' he said. 'We've all got used to food being so cheap, which is the death knell for any small enterprise.

'Having said that, if you did want to do it you could maximize your income by growing high value crops, which are also highly perishable, such as fresh herbs or rocket and courgette flowers. Then, if you could find someone to buy them, you would still make a pittance, but it would be less of a pittance. If you plan to grow cauliflowers and potatoes, you might as well stay in bed.'

GETTING CRAFTY 10

Growing veg and raising chickens is one thing, but what's a self-sufficient person to do when the last decent serving dish in the house breaks or the winter jumper gets threadbare? In order to keep their happy home ticking along, Barbara and Tom were forced to learn new skills, including pottery and weaving, at evening classes. The episode 'A Weaver's Tale' saw Tom blowing his last £10 on an old loom, before realizing that they couldn't get enough wool from Geraldine to make a string vest. Resourceful as ever, he solved the problem by helping out a local farmer in return for some fleeces, raiding the golf course for nettles to make dye and inventing his own crude spindle from wood and string.

   While they didn't go as far as spinning their own wool, Sue and Giles tried their hands at nettle dying, knitting and dressmaking, as well as dabbling in the traditional arts of pottery and whittling.

Dying to go Green

'Man has needs, nature provides,' explained Tom Good, as he emerged from the scrub at Jerry's golf course with an armful of nettles. After spinning the wool they earned from a local sheep farmer, in 'Suit Yourself' Tom and Barbara set about making a 'bilious green' dye from the stinging weed. The end of the episode saw the couple invited to stay for a drink with 'Sir' at a swanky restaurant; Tom removed his coat to reveal a ghastly green, wool suit.

As Barbara explained, green is not the only colour you can achieve with natural dyes: 'You can get yellow from onion skins and brown from walnut shells'. In Scotland, crofters and cottage industries traditionally boiled lichens, scraped from rocks, to produce a variety of colours, including red and purple. The renowned Harris Tweed obtained its distinctive browns and fawns from local lichens called crottle.

Until the 1950s, a majority of garments were manufactured with natural dyes, but advances in technology and the greater demand for cheap clothes means that a bewildering variety of detergents and chemical dyes, including bleach and formaldehyde, are now used in the process. While you may not want everything in your wardrobe to be 'bilious green', clothes made with natural dyes, used on organic cotton and wool sourced from ethical farming, are available if you are prepared to pay a little extra for your fashion.

Making Nettle Dye

Only natural, untreated fibres can be coloured with natural dyes so don't try turning your nylon running shorts into the latest green fashion item.

1. Prepare the clothing by soaking it in a fixative or 'mordant' – a natural chemical that gives the dye something to fix on to. The easiest accessible mordants are vinegar, caustic soda or stale urine – Sue and Giles steered clear of the latter for their attempt! Ideal mordants are alum, tin and copper. Use four parts water to one part mordant. Leave for 30 minutes.

2. Prepare the vegetable dye by boiling chopped nettles in a large pan. Bring to the boil and simmer for one hour, then strain.

3. Drop fabric into the strained dye. The liquid should be warm (if it cools, heat it up again).

4. Stir in the fabric then leave for one hour.

5. Take out the fabric, drain and hang to dry.

'Basically all our clothes look like we've peed ourselves in them. It would have been cheaper and easier just to urinate on them.'

'I can safely say it is the best dress I've ever made.'

'I looked a little bit like a Paisley Gandalf, but it was a good effort I have to say. I can't take credit for it because it was Giles' design and I merely realized it when I got to the sewing machine. He is the John Galliano of north London.'

Giles Turns Dress Designer

Real Good Lifers have an essential 'make do and mend' mentality and Barbara was a dab hand with a needle and thread. She cheerfully turned Tom's old jumper into leg warmers and a tabard, as well as transforming her evening dress into a short frock after ripping the hem.

After weeks in denim dungarees, Sue was yearning for a new look and Giles was on hand to help out – with a novel approach to dressmaking. 'Sue lay on the floor like something out of CSI Surbiton and I cut round her,' he explained. 'I cut it quite close to her famously svelte and elfin form, but then if you cut another bit the same there's no allowance for the elements in which Sue raises out of the second dimension.'

'I'm basically one of the few women that Giles has met that has the third dimension,' joked Sue.

Getting the Needle

As Barbara and Tom had little in the way of spare cash, their gifts to Margo and Jerry in the classic Christmas special 'It's Silly, But It's Fun' were hideous, yellow, home-knitted jumpers that were several sizes too big. For Sue, knitting was not a new experience, but she welcomed the input of experts Susan Ritchie and Karen Miller, who started their own haberdashery shop, Mrs Moon, after returning to the hobby a few years ago. Although Sue is adept at the complicated job of knitting socks with four needles, the simpler patterns, using two needles, proved more difficult and the jumper she started knitting for Giles looked like it was going the same way as Barbara's efforts.

'I like a bit of knitting, nothing wrong with that,' she revealed. 'It's one of the second best ways to go cross-eyed. The ladies were very sweet and I am making Giles a sweater, which is a god-awful creation he will never wear.'

Knitting would seem a useful skill for a self-sufficient lifestyle, and in the seventies would have been essential. However, Susan suggests that one vital change in the last 40 years makes it less viable today.

'Knitting is really back in vogue, but in the seventies people did it to save money because the yarn was cheap. Back then, the yarn was horrible – a lot of polyester and not a lot of sheep – but it was really economical, and people knitted for that reason. It's turned on its head somewhat and most of the younger people who are knitting now are buying really expensive yarn because there is a lot of beautiful stuff out there and some really lovely, modern patterns.

'You still have the traditional knitters at the cheap end, but to be honest these days we have so many chain stores that sell mass-produced clothes at knockdown prices, it's actually more expensive to knit your own. Those of us who knit now really do it for individuality and to get something of a really high quality. You would spend upward of £60 to make one jumper, but it would be a jumper that would cost you £200 or more in a designer outlet.

'I wouldn't want to put all that time and effort into making something that was 100 per cent polyester. I want the best wool available, so the mind-set has changed significantly since the seventies.'

Celebrity knitters, such as Gwyneth Paltrow, Julia Roberts and Madonna, have helped bring the clickety-click of the needles back into vogue, and Susan believes it is a great antidote to the stresses of modern life.

'It's definitely a stress-buster and that's why many people do it. I sit in the evening in front of the television and I do quite a lot of crocheting, but if you'd told me a few years ago that I would be doing this, I wouldn't have believed you. Now I have kids and the shop and I can sit in front of the television in the evening with my crocheting and unwind. It's also a good way to keep off temptations in the evenings, like food, drink or cigarettes. It is actually alarmingly addictive – you finish a project and you can get quite antsy and fidgety until you get your next knitting fix.'

'I made Giles a lovely tank top, which has a canary-yellow chest so he looks like a goldfinch in it. He loved it because it made him look ripped!'

'As soon as I put it on I was tempted to sing in a high-pitched note and crap on the wing.'

Susan's Tips for Beginners

There is a set out there of competitive knitters, who take it to another level and totally intimidate others who are starting,' Susan advises. 'You look at a pattern and think, Oh my God!, and can be put off. So the worst problem for a beginner is a lack of confidence. Just think to yourself, It's only knitting. What's the worst that can happen? Initially, everyone drops stitches and that sort of thing and you need to learn how to remedy those mistakes.

'Start simple with a scarf. Get a big pair of needles, big chunky yarn and you can knit a scarf from scratch, even if you've never knitted before, in about four hours. Then you will have something you will actually wear because the yarn you can get now is really nice. Even if you are not doing anything fancy it comes out as a really beautiful texture so it's a good starter project.'

Going Potty

After signing up to house maintenance classes at the local college, in Series Two the Goods decided to learn a second skill each, with Barbara opting for pottery and Tom for weaving. Margo decided to join her friend at the pottery class and with typical enthusiasm filled the garden shed with expensive equipment before attending a single lesson. She then dropped the class after the instructor 'stared unashamedly' at her breasts, leading Jerry to moan, 'There's £200 worth of electric kiln out in our shed – what's it to become? A monument to one of your tantrums?'

The introduction of small electric kilns was, in fact, one of the reasons for an upsurge in home pottery studios in the seventies. Pottery was routinely taught in schools and evening classes were hugely popular.

Potter Geoffrey Kenward, who took his wheel to north London to show our Good Lifers a thing or two, started teaching in the 1970s and hails the decade as 'the golden age' of pottery.

'In the Good Life scenario they would have gone for the home kiln, about the size of a dustbin. They were an American invention, stainless steel clad – you could easily buy one and put it in the back of your car without any trouble.

'I fire with gas whereas Margo would have fired electrically. That was part of the revolution. People started to make electric kilns in the twenties and thirties, but in the seventies people were producing them in a size that you could have at home.'

By the end of the decade Geoffrey was so much in demand that he was teaching one daytime and three evening classes, often to middle-class housewives like Margo. As Jerry angrily pointed out to Margo, it wasn't cheap to set up a studio, and in that respect it hasn't changed.

'These days you could buy an electric wheel,' explains Geoff. 'A small one – like the Shimpo or the American equivalent – will set you back about £600 to £700. You can buy cheaper wheels, but frankly they're no good. You can go right up to £2000 for a Fitzwilliam wheel like the one we were using. As they are controlled electronically, you can set the acceleration and

'I made a hummous plate, which is very useful – especially if you're Moroccan and short of crockery. It started off as a vase, then became flatter and flatter, but it now has a ridge where you can artfully arrange your hummous. Or tzatziki. Or any other vegetable slop-based starter. Do you know, I think I've found a gap in the market!

'I was enjoying it, but anything I can't immediately do just annoys me. I felt a slight panic when I put my foot on the gas because it reminded me of driving lessons and having to remember to change gear, and steer, while using the windscreen wipers and looking backwards.'

deceleration, which is why they cost a lot more, but it means you can work standing up, and you can throw a really big pot. You can even stand on a ladder if you like.

'Margo's wheel was a kick wheel, which is foot operated, and I've actually got an identical model in my studio. A kick wheel is reasonably cheap these days – probably £300 new and dirt cheap second hand – because most people want power wheels.

'Then you need a small kiln. They vary in price, but you could still pay up to £1000 for one of those. You also need a controller, which is a piece of machinery that controls how fast the kiln fires, how quickly the temperature increases or decreases and turns it off. A really cheap one is around £300, but you would probably want to pay about £500 to £600. So it adds up.'

On top of that there are sponges and buckets, tools and bats, which sit on the wheel to help you take your pot off. Add electricity and clay and you may find yourself potless before you even start.

Margo's faint heart was matched only by Barbara's determination and after weeks of classes she brought home two mashed coffee cups, which Tom christened 'dis' and 'aster'. 'As long as they are functional it doesn't matter what they look like,' he declared, before discovering that one of them leaked. When they swapped classes, however, Tom excelled at pottery and soon had his own cottage industry operating in Margo's shed.

For Giles and Sue, the roles were reversed. The two brave souls squeezed into a tiny shed to try their hand at the potter's wheel and, despite much teasing from her TV partner, Sue found the experience 'mellow' and managed to throw a passable pot. Giles didn't fare quite so well, but, like many first-time potters, he managed to make something resembling an ashtray.

GETTING PRACTICAL

Throwing a Pot

1. Prepare your clay by making sure it is even in texture and there are no hard bits in it.

2. Roll the clay into a ball, without trapping any air, then place it on the very centre of the spinning wheel head.

3. Centre the clay by pushing it gently until it is absolutely in the middle. If it's not in the middle your pot will be a disaster. Keep the clay wet, but not too wet, by dipping your hand in water between handling.

4. Open up the clay by putting your thumb on the top, then push down and pull it across the bottom, to make the bottom of the pot.

5. Pull up or lift the clay with one hand inside and the other outside. Determine the distance between the fingers on the inside and the finger on the outside or 'the trigger' and then move that distance, keeping it even all the way up the pot. This movement pulls the pot wall up. Do it two or three times until you achieve the thickness you want.

6. Fashion the pot into the shape you want by pushing outward from the inside.

7. Allow the pot to dry until it becomes cheesy, or 'leather hard'. Use turning tools to turn away the excess clay and shape the pot further. Then decorate and glaze.

Firing

1. Dry the pot completely. 'If it's not bone dry, it blows up,' explains Geoff. 'Drying will take a week in a shed or two to three days in the house.'

2. Place the pot in the kiln. If you have more than one don't worry if they touch each other.

3. Fire very slowly to get all the remaining moisture out.

4. Fire it up to about 1000ºC (1830ºF). This process is called bisque (or biscuit) firing, and comes from the French term meaning fired twice.

5. At the end of the firing, cool it down and glaze in a bucket of water and glaze powder.

6. Put the pot back in the kiln and fire fast, either to the same temperature if it is earthenware or higher, at least 1200ºC (2200ºF), for stoneware.

7. The pottery is now vitreous, meaning the particles of clay have melted together to form a sort of glass, so it is no longer porous. You don't actually need to glaze it, but it will look nicer and be easier to clean if you do.

8. Cool it down slowly. If you cool too quickly the pot will suffer from 'dunting', which means it will split and break.

Woodwork

In order to run a self-sufficient plot, woodworking is an essential skill. From fashioning your own tools to building animal stalls and hen houses, the ability to knock something together will save a smallholder a small fortune. Traditional craftsman Guy Mallinson was on hand to show Giles and Sue the fundamentals of green woodworking, or working with unseasoned wood. He brought with him a pole lathe, which spins the wood as it is cut, sanded or drilled so that it can be carved into bowls and candlesticks, and a shaving horse, which holds the wood in place as it is shaved.

'We made a spatula for cooking and something that resembled a dibber, for planting,' Guy explains. 'They're not the easiest things to make, but they seemed the most relevant, as cooking and planting are important jobs for the self-sufficient home. The problem is that it usually takes about two days to get up to speed and we only had a couple of hours so they ended up with a half-finished dibber and a half-finished spatula, but they seemed quite happy with them.'

As well as fronting craft shows on TV, Guy runs woodworking courses in Dorset, but believes a course isn't entirely necessary for the beginner. 'I do everything I can to encourage people to take up making things by hand, particularly in wood. But you don't need to go on a course, you can get a book on whittling, a knife and a stick, and you're off.'

And you don't have to live in the country to take it up as a hobby. Even in the city there is plenty of free wood to be found.

'The spatula was good, but we didn't finish it properly which meant that every time we flipped an egg, 400,000 shards of wood ended up in the yolk. Good if you are a fan of splinter omelette.'

'There's no time to learn such crafts these days, so I enjoyed having a go at woodworking – taking it in turns to operate the pole lathe. It was a great piece of medieval equipment. It's a lovely arcane craft.'

'There are quite a few urban bodgers [green woodworkers]. The trick is to get in touch with the local council tree surgeons who are forever chopping bits off and having to shred them. The park departments are very helpful as well.'

As fewer schools teach traditional crafts, such as woodwork, Guy thinks it is important that children are taught how to use tools responsibly.

'The practice of making crafts is disappearing. When I was a child we were all making corn dollies and the boys even learned sewing at school. We made things.

'I think it's a great shame that kids aren't being given the chance to learn these skills, and they are skills everyone should learn. When you become skilled at woodwork, if you need something quickly you can cobble it together rather than resorting to buying it – that's essential for a self-supporting family.'

PART FOUR
CHRISTMAS

HAPPY HOMEMADE CHRISTMAS 11

The Christmas episode of *The Good Life* is one of the most memorable of the four series. On Christmas Eve, Barbara was busy making newspaper chain robins, dubbed 'little Christmas vultures' by Tom, and a papier-mâché version of the Yule log. To accompany Barbara's paper creations, Tom brought in holly and mistletoe he had pinched from the golf course and a tiny Christmas tree top, which he had been given by the local greengrocer after it fell off the top of a pine. With homemade crackers and presents, the only shop-bought item for their Christmas celebrations was a packet of balloons, costing 15p.

Next door, Margo was in high dudgeon when the 9ft tree she had ordered turned out to be 6in too short. As Tom marvelled, 'Your Christmas comes in a van,' she sent her entire order back, only to be left without a decoration, a morsel of food or a drop of wine on Christmas Day.

Goodwill to all Men

Despite Tom's quip that 'It's all getting very commercial' on totting up the 15p cost for balloons, Christmas in the seventies was far less commercialized than it is today. Most people saw it as a short break from work and a chance to see family and friends.

The percentage of UK families regularly attending church has fallen by 40 per cent since the seventies and for many people the festive season has more to do with buying gifts and stocking up on party food than celebrating the birth of Christ. With the aim of avoiding these modern day costs, Giles and Sue set about making their own decorations, cards and gifts – unfortunately, with disappointing results.

'I didn't really make anything of note. I made some potato prints that turned out like the Star of David, so there were a lot of weirdly Jewish Christmas cards,' revealed Sue. 'When it comes to the artistic things it's fair to say that neither of us covered ourselves in glory. There were a lot of dud Christmas cards going out to neighbours who warranted more, considering our goats had crapped all over their front garden for the last two months and the turkeys kept them awake all night.'

Giles also found their potato printing efforts risible. 'Potato printing is a byword for entry level education,' he quipped. 'I've always joked about leaving school without getting much past potato printing, but actually I can't even potato print.'

'I made the greatest, truest, most tear-jerkingly accurate statue of a robin on a log out of three lumps of plasticine, in four seconds. After that it was all downhill.'

Making Christmas Crackers

Tom and Barbara's crackers may not have made the right noise when they were pulled, but with a little improvisation they made the party go with a bang. Margo refused to wear her hat because it was made out of the *Daily Mirror*, but cheered up when Tom swapped it for a *Telegraph* version. Here's how to make your own:

You will need:
Toilet roll tubes for the cracker centre
Colour supplements
Paper
Newspaper hats
Small homemade gifts
Glue
Scissors

1. Make paper hats (see opposite).

2. Cut a piece of plain paper into small strips and write silly jokes on them.

3. Lay a sheet of colour supplement flat out on the table.

4. Fill a loo roll with a joke strip, a paper hat and a gift and place it on the paper.

5. Roll the supplement around the roll and glue along the edge so that it stays wrapped up.

6. Carefully twist each end to seal the cracker.

Making a Newspaper Hat

You will need a newspaper sheet consisting of two pages. Broadsheet size works best, but tabloid can be used for smaller heads.

1. Fold the sheet in half along the natural newspaper crease.

2. Fold in half again the other way, so that the top of the page meets the bottom.

3. Now fold the two top corners towards the middle so that the edges meet. This will make a pointed top.

4. Take the bottom edge of one side and fold up to the bottom of the triangle. Then fold again so it overlaps the triangle part.

5. (If you are using tabloid size, skip this step). Turn the hat over and fold the sides in by 3cm, so that it looks like a house.

6. Fold the bottom strip as in step 4.

Blue Peter Advent Crown

The seventies Christmas wouldn't be the same without the classic *Blue Peter* ensemble, the advent crown. Introduced as a 'Make' in the sixties, it was an annual favourite until 2009 when it was dropped due to health and safety concerns.

Giles and Sue had a visit from *Blue Peter* icon Peter Purves, who presented the show in the golden age between 1968 and 1978. He showed them how to make the famous decoration, which consists of four wire coat hangers tied together with garden twine, decorated with tinsel and with candles placed at each of the four corners. A candle was lit once a week in December to mark the run-up to Christmas.

CHRISTMAS IS A COMIN'
BING CROSBY

Green Christmas

With battery-powered toys, fake Christmas trees, miles of wrapping paper and cupboards and fridges packed with pre-prepared party food and drink imported from all over the world, it's hard to be green at Christmas. But through their attempts at self-sufficiency, Giles and Sue's festive décor was more environmentally friendly than most. They reused old colour supplements and newspapers for wrapping paper and decorations, crackers and Christmas hats. Excess vegetable peelings from the Christmas dinner went to the animals, and could also be turned into compost. Mary Berry supplied Giles and Sue with a turkey to roast, but if they had killed their own turkey to eat with their homegrown vegetables, they could have reduced their food miles further.

One way of staying eco-friendly at Christmas is to buy a real tree from a reputable supplier. As more trees are planted each year to replace the ones cut down, pine farms help reduce carbon emission. If you have the space you could go one step further and grow your own tree in time for Christmas and then recycle it afterwards. Card recycling schemes have sprung up everywhere now too, so never throw old Christmas cards in the bin.

A University of Manchester study recently revealed that by the time it reaches the table, the average British Christmas dinner has travelled 49,000 miles! Buying local produce or growing your own cuts out those food miles and sourcing a local free-range turkey also helps. Also, defrost your freezer just before the festive season – it will work more efficiently and there will be plenty of room for the leftovers.

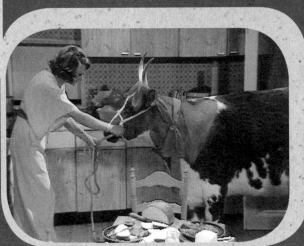

CHRISTMAS COOKING 12

After Harrods wouldn't deliver their order on Christmas Day, Margo phoned her social circle to tell them Jerry had chickenpox and lamented, 'Christmas is cancelled. They won't deliver it.'

In the spirit of the season, Tom and Barbara invited their neighbours to share their Christmas chicken, provided from their own stock, served with potatoes and vegetables from the garden.

After dinner, Jerry noted, 'I must say, your food really does taste like food,' and after throwing herself into the silly games, Margo declared it the best Christmas ever. The programme ended with Christmas gift swapping – two handmade, super-size knitted jumpers for Margo and Jerry and, much to Tom and Barbara's surprise, a cow for them!

A Good Christmas

For the 21st-century Good Lifers, the powers-that-be ensured they enjoyed a white Christmas on their Christmas Day. Old pals Giles and Sue made the most of the snow with a 'friendly' snowball fight, which left Sue a little bruised.

'Giles has a good throw. He's got a mighty aim and I caught one right on the backside.'

'If I'm going to play, I play for keeps!' laughed a remorseless Giles.

Before the turkey dinner, the pair exchanged presents. While Giles opened a home-knitted, canary-yellow tank top, Sue unwrapped a pair of bright red wellies.

'He secretly has a rubber plantation out the back, which I hadn't noticed, and managed to fashion the rubber into a pair of red wellies with the use of cochineal dye,' she joked.

If the snow and presents weren't enough, to create a festive mood, à la Tom and Barbara, Giles and Sue made Christmas-tree biscuits with Sophie Grigson and a Boxing Day chutney, using cranberries and apples, which made a perfect accompaniment for the cold turkey, goat's cheese and pickled eggs.

SOPHIE GRIGSON'S SEASONAL BISCUIT RECIPE

....

Makes a lot!

150g (5oz) golden syrup
110g (4oz) golden caster sugar
1 teaspoon ground cinnamon
1 teaspoon vanilla essence
¼ teaspoon bicarbonate
   of soda
110g (4oz) softened,
   unsalted butter
1 large egg
450g (1lb) plain flour

For the royal icing:
1 egg white
225g (8oz) icing sugar

To decorate:
Icing pens
Silver balls and other edible
   decorations
Ribbon, string or wool

1. Pre-heat the oven to 150°C/300°F/Gas 2.

2. Put the syrup, sugar, cinnamon and vanilla into a heavy saucepan. Stir over a low heat until the sugar has completely dissolved, then bring to the boil. Now stir in the bicarbonate of soda – it will become foamy and very thick. Take the pan off the heat.

3. Immediately, pour the mixture onto the butter in a large bowl and stir until it has all dissolved. Now beat in the egg, then add the flour in four or five batches, beating it in well each time until you have a soft dough. Chill for at least an hour before using.

4. Roll the dough out on a well-floured surface to the thickness of a £1 coin, and then stamp out stars, diamonds, reindeers or whatever other shapes you fancy.

5. Pierce a hole in each one for the ribbon or thread, making it a little larger than you need as the dough will spread slightly as it cooks. Bake on baking sheets lined with non-stick baking parchment for about 20 minutes or until they are as dry as a bone. Leave the biscuits to cool on a wire rack.

6. To make the royal icing, beat the egg white lightly then add enough icing sugar to make a thick icing. Drizzle over the biscuits or decorate with icing pens and colourful edible baubles. Leave to dry, then thread ribbon, string or wool through the hole and knot so that the biscuits can be hung from the tree.

CHRISTMAS CHUTNEY

1kg (2lb) cranberries
1kg (2lb) cooking apples
500g (1lb) onions
500g (1lb) brown sugar
2 teaspoons ground allspice
A pinch each of ground cloves,
   nutmeg, dry mustard and
   cayenne
Juice and grated peel of
   two oranges
25g (1oz) salt
1 litre (1¾ pints) malt vinegar

1. Place the cranberries in a pan with the peeled, cored and chopped apples and the peeled chopped onions.

2. Add the rest of the ingredients and bring to the boil.

3. Simmer until all the liquid has evaporated.

4. Store in a sterilized, tightly sealed jar.

The Truth About Turkeys

Self-sufficiency guru John Seymour was not a huge fan of turkeys when it came to home rearing. 'Compared to other poultry, these are very delicate birds,' he wrote in *The Complete Book of Self-Sufficiency* in 1976. 'If they associate in any way with chickens, they get a fatal disease called Blackhead. You must keep them well away from chickens… It's hardly worth it. Turkeys do not seem to me to be a very suitable bird for the self-supported.'

Barbara and Tom appeared to agree, settling for chicken for their seasonal feast, while the Leadbetters ordered a goose. For the Christmas special, Giles and Sue acquired two free-range turkeys, brought to the house by breeder Paul Kelly. Paul has been breeding turkeys since 1972 and supplies many top outlets and even provides Christmas dinner for the royal family. Paul is a second-generation breeder who uses traditional free-range rearing methods.

'We work on about 300-400 birds per acre,' he explains. 'Our turkeys are free range so they go in and out of sheds but we also have some that are totally wild and live in the woods, as nature intended.' Although they have to be housed separately from other poultry, he believes turkeys are fine birds for the smallholder, providing they can get over the first five weeks.

'They are difficult to rear for the first five weeks because they can be suicidal – they will jump in a bucket of water or sit down and not eat and drink. Chickens will hatch and immediately run around looking for food and water. With a turkey chick, if the food and water isn't there for them to eat as they want, they think, Oh well, I'll just die then.

'Once they get over that bit, they are easy to care for. Chicks costs between £3 and £5; you rear it for six months and then it's ready to eat. The food costs about £8 and in total they'll end up costing about £25, which is still very cheap for a turkey.'

At the house, the two male turkeys were given their own Christmas-themed hut, complete with Christmas tree, and were allowed to wander around the garden as well. Although not destined for the plate on the show, Giles and Sue's turkeys, reared

on Paul's farm, are allowed 6 months to grow before being slaughtered. For factory-farmed birds the growth time is, unsurprisingly, much quicker.

'There are 50-plus breeds of turkey and the modern white turkey will be killed, typically, at 12 or 13 weeks at Christmas.'

If you are breeding your own turkeys, consider a slow-growing breed that gets to 5 kilos (12–13lbs) and will feed an average family. The slow-growing turkey will have a stronger flavoured meat with more fat marbling, meaning that it will cook more quickly while remaining moist.

One thing that hasn't changed since the seventies is the supposed need for a long cooking for this festive bird. Paul thinks it's time to move on.

'Most turkeys are cremated at Christmas, unfortunately,' he says. 'The long cooking period came about in the era of the frozen turkey in the sixties and seventies, when people were paranoid about salmonella poisoning. Hygiene has moved on enormously, but the old cooking instructions have stuck. Turkey is not a very forgiving meat. If it is overcooked it can be very dry and bland, but if you get it right it is delicious.

'The turkeys were very loud and they woke the neighbours up at four in the morning. They were quite good-humoured about it. I would have gone out and wrung the turkeys' necks. But, as usual with our livestock, they were not destined for the table. They were just destined to get older and noisier.'

PAUL KELLY'S EIGHT STEPS TO THE PERFECT CHRISTMAS TURKEY

....

Allow two hours of cooking time for a 4kg (8lb) bird. For each extra kg add 15 minutes.

1. Remove the bird from the fridge, leave it to stand at room temperature for 2 hours before cooking.

2. Preheat the oven to 180°C/350°F/Gas 4.

3. Place the turkey, breast down, in a roasting tin and season the back of the bird with salt and pepper. Most of the fat deposits are on the back of the bird and these will percolate through the breast, allowing the turkey to cook in its own juices.

4. Place a large peeled onion in the cavity for extra flavour. Do not use tin foil, as the skin will be steamed instead of crispy.

5. Turn the turkey over (to brown the breast) 30 minutes before then end of cooking time. This is easily done by holding the end of the drumsticks with oven gloves (be careful of hot fat).

6. Use a meat thermometer to test when the turkey is cooked. Insert the thermometer halfway through the thickest part of the breast. The temperature should reach 70°C (137°F) for more than 2 minutes. If it doesn't, put the turkey back in the oven and check every 10 minutes until the correct temperature is reached.

7. If you don't have a meat thermometer, insert a skewer into the thigh and when the juices run clear remove the bird from the oven. If the juices are pink, place it back in the oven and keep checking it at 10 minute intervals.

8. Allow to stand for 30 to 60 minutes before carving.

A Berry Merry Christmas

Barbara and Tom may have cooked a wonderful roast in their rusty, old wood-burning stove, but the prospect of producing a full Christmas feast in their somewhat temperamental stove was a daunting prospect for our modern-day Good Lifers.

Ever keen on expert advice, Giles and Sue called in Aga queen Mary Berry to help tackle the turkey. The celebrated chef, whose first book was published in 1966 and since then has written over 70 more, has sold more than five million books worldwide. She specializes in family food and solid fuel stoves, and the *Mail on Sunday* once declared, 'Mary Berry is to Aga what Pavarotti is to opera'.

To go with the roast turkey, Mary cooked red cabbage, lemon and thyme stuffing and bread sauce.

MARY BERRY'S CHRISTMAS RECIPES

···························

Slow-Cooked Red Cabbage

Knob of butter
1 large onion, thinly sliced
1kg (2lb) red cabbage, finely shredded
1 cooking apple, peeled, cored and thinly sliced
4 tablespoons light brown sugar
2 tablespoons white wine vinegar
2 tablespoons redcurrant jelly

1. Preheat the oven to 180°C/350°F/Gas 4. Melt the butter in a large frying pan. Add the onion and fry for a few minutes over a high heat.

2. Wash the cabbage in a colander, then add to the pan.

3. Add apple, sugar, vinegar and redcurrant jelly and bring to the boil. Stir and season with salt and pepper.

4. Cover and transfer to the oven for about 1½–2 hours until the cabbage is tender. Serve hot or cold.

'Mary Berry is very lovely and sweet and a wonderful cook, and the stuffing was very good indeed. The turkey turned out better than it would have done under the auspices of Sue or me, but it's quite a hard thing to cook in a solid fuel stove when you can't control the temperature.'

Lemon and Thyme Pork Stuffing

25g (1oz) butter
1 small onion, chopped
450g (1lb) pork sausagemeat
50g (2oz) fresh white
   breadcrumbs
Finely grated zest and juice
   of half a large lemon
2 tablespoons chopped
   fresh parsley
Leaves from three sprigs
   fresh thyme
Salt and freshly ground
   black pepper

1. Fry the onion in the butter until lightly caramelized.

2. Combine the sausagemeat, breadcrumbs, onion, lemon zest and juice and herbs and mix well.

3. Season with salt and pepper then stuff into the neck cavity of the turkey.

Bread Sauce

1 onion, quartered
4 cloves
2 bay leaves
450ml (15fl oz) fresh
   whole goat's milk
100g (4oz) fresh white
   breadcrumbs
25g (1oz) butter
Salt and freshly ground
   black pepper
A little grated nutmeg

1. Bring the milk to a gentle simmer.

2. Stud the onion with the cloves and add to the milk along with the bay leaves and bring to the boil.

3. Take off the heat and allow the milk to stand for at least 15–20 minutes (or longer if you have time), to allow the flavours to infuse.

4. Discard the onion and bay leaves then stir in the breadcrumbs and heat through.

5. Add the butter and leave on a very low heat, stirring now and then, until the sauce has thickened.

6. Season with salt and pepper and a little nutmeg, if desired.

'The problem is that it takes ages to get to the right oven temperature. As soon as you do, you put the bird in, but the oven continues to get hotter and hotter and suddenly the gauge goes up and you've basically nuked the outside and the inside is still raw.'

Christmas Cocktails and Canapes

A seventies Christmas wouldn't be complete without a Margo and Jerry-style cocktail party. Thanks to the non-delivery of their hamper, Margo was forced to cancel all her entertaining, but Sue and Giles gathered a few famous faces from seventies TV to share a cocktail – and a can of condensed soup. *Tiswas* star Sally James, *Doctor Who* beauty Louise Jameson and *The Goodies* icon Tim Brooke-Taylor all popped in for a Gin Fizz, while *Swap Shop* presenter Keith Chegwin stuck to the virgin cocktails.

'Unfortunately we drank all the cocktail spirits before the guests arrived and then were unable to serve anything except Gin Fizz,' joked Sue. 'We drank a bottle of advocaat, half a bottle of gin, half a bottle of vodka and a tin of beef consommé before they'd even arrived.'

The beef consommé, a clear, tinned soup, was a genuine cocktail ingredient in the seventies and Giles viewed the array of ingredients before him with some suspicion.

'You look at the trolley and see a bottle of advocaat, beef consommé, maraschino cherries and a soda siphon and you think, What on earth am I supposed to make with that? That's not the ingredients for a drink.'

'Sue's Margo is fantastic. It's quite chilling. When I hear her calling "Jerry", I feel the same chill in my bones that I'm sure Paul Eddington did.'

'We did a Margo and Jerry tea party, which involved getting hammered and talking about Margaret Thatcher.'

'You actually make a Bullshot with beef consommé, vodka and lemon juice. If you made a good-quality, clear beef consommé and put a shot of vodka in it, I imagine it could be nice in cold weather. But the cold, canned beef soup we had on our drinks trolley with a slug of alcohol in it was not the same.'

In their Margo and Jerry personas, Giles and Sue also threw a tea party to discuss the politics of the seventies with newshound John Sergeant and author Alwyn Turner. Like many seventies suburbanites, Margo was a staunch Conservative in the time that Margaret Thatcher was the leader of the opposition, and made frequent references to 'the state of this country' under the Labour government. Alwyn Turner suggested a connection between Margo and Margaret Thatcher as 'a suburban hat-wearing lady, a woman who could have been Margo Leadbetter's other next-door neighbour', although he did point out that the Iron Lady thrived on breaking the rules of the 'boys' club' mentality.

For his part, Giles was amused as Sue took on the mantel of the respectable Tory housewife.

'It's funny watching Sue trying to be a really dour Thatcherite,' he said. 'I like to see that square peg in that round hole. Sue is always first to occupy the socio-political high ground but was forced to relinquish it for the sake of the character.'

Cocktail Hour

Giles and Sue mixed up a few classic seventies combinations at their cocktail party, taken from Arabella Boxer's 1975 book *Christmas Food and Drink*, some with rather unusual ingredients for modern tastebuds:

Black Velvet: Dry champagne and stout.

Bullshot: Tinned beef consommé and vodka.

Pink Gin Fizz: Gin, sugar syrup and angostura bitters.

Snowball: Advocaat, lemonade and lime cordial.

THE VERDICT: WAS IT GOOD FOR YOU?

As the summer drew to a close, Sue and Giles sat down to their final meal in the Good Life house. The animals had survived the experiment at Sue's behest but she made a tasty vegetarian pie to make up for it – despite their part-time horticultural efforts they were left with a wide variety of produce.

As they ate their last supper in the garden, the pair found they had become converts to many of the ideas of self-sufficiency.

'I was pretty sceptical that you could produce much from a London garden or an urban environment, but I have been proved totally wrong,' admitted Sue. 'I thought we'd grow crap vegetables but they tasted really good. I made terrible pastry but the quality of the vegetables is so much better than from the supermarket and that's coming out of a small London garden. And we weren't even very good. Imagine if someone was naturally very good at this, and they worked the soil and made it fertile – it would be fabulous, especially if you have kids.

'Kids get so excited about pulling the muddy top of a carrot and hearing it pop as it comes out of the ground. My nieces used to come down to Cornwall in the summer to help me harvest the vegetables that I grew in my garden and they were way more excited about it than they were about any computer game. It's so much more interactive, it gives them a better understanding, and the growing can be done on a small scale.'

As a committed townie, the experience was a steep learning curve for Giles but, having recently married, he is now looking forward to dabbling in grow-your-own with a future generation of Corens.

'When I have children I won't bother with a silly garden full of flowers,' he promised. 'I'll grow vegetables and I will have chickens or something a bit smaller – quails perhaps. People know less and less about where the food they eat comes from and I think it would be really nice for children to grow up with that. At the moment, I have the sort of garden with herbaceous borders that the kids are going to tear to pieces playing football, so I can imagine that within three years all the flower beds will be out and I will have a vegetable patch, six chickens and a trampoline!'

For Sue the aesthetics of a suburban garden were improved by the addition of animals and vegetable patches and she would like to see more homeowners swapping some of their flowers for more practical plants.

'I think that when a garden is in full swing with all the vegetables and animals it is so much more beautiful,' she said. 'I think we've got into this idea that unless a garden has concrete for the car and borders full of pretty little pink flowers that it's not beautiful. I like wilderness and I just think it's sometimes fantastic to forget all the Victorian claptrap about trying to control nature and let nature control you for a bit. It's really liberating. Just stick some plants in, watch them thrive and relax about it.

'It's not about pruning and dead-heading and organising, it's about working together with nature.'

Having confessed to a fear of the animals around his childhood holiday home in the New Forest, Giles was surprised to find himself warming to his furry and feathered companions.

'For me the animals were the best thing and the goats were a real revelation,' he marvelled. 'If I could get to like goat's milk as much as I like normal milk, I definitely think a goat would be a lovely thing to keep. I probably wouldn't do it in London, as you'd have to have a bit more space, but goats are much more useful than pets. I'm not an animal lover like Sue and I don't want a dog, but I'd love to have a goat. Having freshly laid eggs was also a marvel – a potato straight out of the ground is quite nice but it tastes the same as a potato from a good vegetable shop. A fresh egg, however, is a fresh egg and it tastes wonderful.'

Even so, both presenters accept that a total switch to self-sufficiency, in the style of Tom and Barbara, is no easy task, particularly in the confines of a suburban garden.

'Complete self-sufficiency wouldn't work with that garden,' Giles concluded. 'The space is too small, we never had any great success with the vegetables and you need some small form of income. A couple could achieve it, if one of you could work part-time to bring in some money. I'm a writer, so I could write for two days a week and tend to my little home farm in between. It is a wonderful thing to do but if you don't have any other form of income you will end up like farmers throughout history, with seven fat years and seven lean. You could get very depressed when it doesn't work and it's a question of whether the good days will see you through the bad ones. No modern, working urban professional is temperamentally suited to that but the point is that you can change yourself.'

Sue believes that starting with small changes, which easily fit into your lifestyle, is the way to success.

'What I learned is that it's about balance,' she said. 'I would never go into being totally self-sufficient because it's a full-time job, and I have a full-time job that I really love. It's about trying some new things. Start small, work out what's right for you, and what your lifestyle can accommodate. If you want to go away on holiday, don't get pigs. Instead, try growing vegetables.

'I really got into making cheese, which I never thought I would, so I will definitely be giving that a go again. This is about living the "Good Life", taking things from nature that make you feel better and more alive. It's not about exchanging one form of nine-to-five drudgery for another. I don't believe it has to be a totalitarian shift from the supermarket to growing your own, but if you can take some of the slack and if you can grow some produce and buy locally and seasonally to cut down on trips to the supermarket, you'd be solving a major environmental crisis right there. A few small changes can make all the difference.'

On the question of truly living a self-sufficient life, Giles pondered, 'I wouldn't miss television, although I would have to have a wind-up radio to listen to the cricket. What I would miss most is hot water and my car, and drinking good wine. Having goats was great but I would probably miss cow products, like milk and steak. But you'd only need slightly more land, then you could have a cow.

'This was a first try and we went into it not knowing a lot so we were finding out about it all as we went along. As with anything you do for the first time, whether it be redecorating a bathroom or getting the builders in, you learn lessons and you know not to do certain things next time. It's a bigger version of that. Knowing what I know now, it would be a lot easier next time.'

USEFUL RESOURCES

General

www.accidentalsmallholder.net

Wood-burning stoves

www.solidfuel.co.uk

www.hetas.co.uk

www.planningportal.gov.uk

www.smokecontrol.defra.gov.uk

Department for Environment,
Food and Rural Affairs (Defra),
Air Quality Policy Division,
Zone 4/D13, Ashdown House,
123 Victoria Street, London
SW1E 6DE

Animal husbandry

Defra
www.defra.gov.uk
Tel: 08459 33 55 77

Rural Payments Agency
www.rpa.gov.uk
Tel: 0845 603 7777
Food Standards Agency
(for approved slaughterhouses
and advice on selling meat)
www.food.gov.uk
General helpline tel: 020 7276 8829

British Goat Society
www.allgoats.com
Tel:01434 240 866

British Pig Association
www.britishpigs.org
Tel: 01223 845 100

Poultry World Magazine
www.poultryworld.org

Practical Poultry magazine website
www.practicalpoultry.co.uk

Smallholder Magazine
www.smallholder.co.uk

Wine and cider laws

www.hmrc.gov.uk

Eco fuel

Energy Saving Trust
www.energysavingtrust.org.uk
Tel: 0800 512 012

Beekeeping

The British Beekeepers' Association
www.britishbee.org.uk

INDEX

Index

This book is published to accompany the television series entitled *Giles and Sue Live the Good Life*, first broadcast on BBC TWO in 2010.

silver river

Executive Producers: Dan Adamson & Daisy Goodwin
Series Producer: Lucy Hooper
Series Director: Neil Ferguson

10 9 8 7 6 5 4 3 2 1

Published in 2010 by BBC Books, an imprint of Ebury Publishing. A Random House Group Company

The Random House Group Limited Reg. No. 954009

Addresses for companies within the Random House Group can be found at www.randomhouse.co.uk

A CIP catalogue record for this book is available from the British Library.

ISBN 978 1 849 90059 1

Mixed Sources
Product group from well-managed forests and other controlled sources
www.fsc.org   Cert no. SGS-COC-005091
© 1996 Forest Stewardship Council

The Random House Group Limited supports the Forest Stewardship Council (FSC), the leading international forest certification organisation. All our titles that are printed on Greenpeace approved FSC certified paper carry the FSC logo. Our paper procurement policy can be found at www.rbooks.co.uk/environment

Commissioning editor: Lorna Russell
Project editor: Laura Higginson
Copy-editor: Wendy Hollas
Design and illustrations: Smith & Gilmour
Photographer: Sarah Cuttle
Production: David Brimble

Colour origination by: XY Digital
Printed and bound in UK by Butler Tanner & Dennis

To buy books by your favourite authors and register for offers, visit www.rbooks.co.uk

TEXT AND PHOTOGRAPHY CREDITS
Photography and text © Woodlands Books 2010

With the exception of recipes/step-by-step methods appearing on pages 57 (© Joe Swift), 60–61 and 196 (© Sophie Grigson/*The Vegetable Bible*/Harper Collins), 100 (© Rosemary Schrager), 108 (© John Seymour/*The Complete Book of Self Sufficiency*/ Dorling Kindersley), 115 (© C. J. J. Berry), 119 (© Bob Flowerdew), 198 (© 2008 Readers Digest Association, Inc./*Food From Your Garden & Allotment* p249, 203 (© Kelly Bronze), 204 and 207 (© Mary Berry/*Mary Berry's Christmas Collection*/ Headline Publishing Group Ltd).

And photography used on pages 38 (© Linda Burgess/ Garden Picture Library), 54–55 (© Maxine Adcock, Frederic Didillion and Francoise De Heel/Garden Picture Library), 68 (© Animal Photography), 74 (© British Goat Society and Animal Photography), 82 (© Charles Sainsbury-Plaice and Animal Photography), 139 (© Glenn Dearing), 150 (© Malgorzata Kistryn/ Shutterstock), 153 (top right © Robert Canis), 201 (© FoodPhotography Eising/Getty).

While every effort has been made to trace and acknowledge all contributors, we should like to apologise should there be any errors or omissions.

ACKNOWLEDGEMENTS
BBC Books would like to thank Giles Coren and Sue Perkins for taking up the fascinating self-sufficiency challenge, and all the knowledgeable contributors to this book for their time and expertise, especially James Greig and Charlotte White for their invaluable help in research. Thanks too to Daisy Goodwin and Dan Adamson at Silver River and also to Lucy Hooper and Neil Ferguson for their patience, as well as to Beccy Green and Imogen Greenslade and commissioning executive Lisa Edwards at BBC. And many thanks to Alison Maloney for her hard work, patience and dedication, Sarah Cuttle for the wonderful photography, Wendy Hollas, Lara Maiklem and Lisa Footit and Smith & Gilmour for designing this thoroughly entertaining and practical book.